Pavel Pushin

DIARIES

OF

THE 1812-1814 CAMPAIGNS

Translated by Alexander Mikaberidze

Tbilisi, Georgia

2011

TABLE OF CONTENTS

PREFACE

Russia had played a decisive role in the Napoleonic Wars and the success in the struggle against the Napoleonic France allowed the Russian leaders to shape the course of European history. Yet Russian voices are oftentimes absent from the pages of historical accounts since a combination of political and ideological rivalries, linguistic difficulties and administrative hurdles created a substantial dearth of English translations of Russian narratives of the Napoleonic Wars. As of today, only a handful of Russian memoirs is available to the Western audience, even though there are dozens of memoirs and diaries illustrating Russian experiences of the Napoleonic Wars. To commemorate the 200th anniversaries of the Napoleonic Wars, the "Russian Voice of the Napoleonic Wars" series will gradually present previously unknown or unavailable Russian primary sources to the Western audience.

The first installment in the series is the diary of Pavel Pushin (1789-1865), Russian Guard officer and participant of the Napoleonic Wars. Pushin was born into the Russian noble family from the Pskov province, where his father served as an actual state councilor. The family was considered well to do since his record of service refers to an estate of 160 serfs. As a result, Pushin was enrolled into the prestigious Page Corps at the young age of eight (28 August 1797) and received a well rounded education, becoming fluent in French and German and demonstrating abilities in arithmetic, geometry, algebra, history, geography and drawing. On 22 January 1801, he obtained a position of kammer-page at the Imperial court and a year later began military service as an ensign in the elite Life Guard Semeyonovskii Regiment (16 November 1802). He served with this regiment throughout the Napoleonic Wars, earning promotion to a sub-lieutenant on 21 August 1805, lieutenant on 29 August 1807, staff captain on 20 February 1809 and to captain on 13 May 1811. Along the way, he distinguished himself in the battles at Austerlitz (awarded the Order of St. Anna, 3rd class) and Borodino (awarded the Order of St. Vladimir, 4th class with ribbon). In 1813, he received the rank of a colonel (1 February 1813) and served with distinction at Lutzen, Bautzen, Pirna, Kulm (received a golden sword for courage and the "Kulm Cross") and Leipzig. On 1 November 1813, he was appointed as a battalion commander of the Life Guard Semeyonovskii Regiment and participated in the crossing of the Rhine and the subsequent campaign in France and occupation of Paris.

After the end of the Napoleonic Wars, he was appointed commander of the Okhotskii Infantry Regiment in January 1816 but, in April, was transferred to command the Neishlotskii Infantry Regiment deployed in Moldavia. Promoted to a major general on 13 May 1818, he commanded the 2nd Brigade of the 16th Division for three years, receiving commendations for his meritorious service.

The 1813-1814 Campaigns in Germany and France had a profound impact on Pushin who witnessed how different life was in Europe compared to Russia and, upon returning home, he became a member of newly emerging Russian liberal secret societies in 1815-1818 and established a Free Masons Lodge in Chisinau in early 1821. He became prominent in liberal circles, was on good terms with the celebrated Russian poet Alexander Pushkin, who dedicated one of his poems to Pushin.

In March 1821, Pushin retired from military service. Officially, his retirement was caused by his poor health and the commander-in-chief of the 2nd Army General Peter Wittgenstein's report to Emperor Alexander spoke of Pushin's "chest pains threatening to develop into consumption and requiring treatments at the spas in Seltzer, Teplitz and Baden." But some scholars also suggest that Pushin's involvement with the secret societies drew attention of the government, forcing him to retire early. Living at his estate, Pushin took no part in the Decembrist Revolt in 1825 but his name was mentioned in conversations of the Decembrist leaders which brought additional government scrutiny to the disgraced general. Pushin spent the next forty years of his life leaving a secluded life at his estate. Russia's defeat in the Crimean War (1854-1856) deeply affected him and, in later years, he was glad to see some of his liberal ideas come to fruition as Emperor Alexander II implemented the Great Reforms in early 1860s. Pushin died in Odessa on 31 July 1865.

Starting in 1812, Pushin maintained a daily record of his campaigns in a diary which eventually covered the last three years of the Napoleonic Wars. The diary is remarkable for the immediacy of events described in it. Reading it, we can envision Pushin, tired from constant marching he was subjected to, sitting in his tent or on a rare occasion in a small room, and writing about his experiences and impressions under the feeble light of a candle. His diary may occasionally seem rather monotonous to a modern reader but it does contain valuable insights into the characters of Russian generals and officers and realities of campaigning, relations within the ranks as well as the outside world.

The diary is quite well known in Russian historical circles and went through three editions. The first edition appeared in a small newspapers *"Za tsarya i Rodinu"* in Odessa in 1908.[1] Four years later an abridged version of the diary was printed in a compilation of documents related to the regimental history of the Life Guard Semeyonovskii Regiment.[2] The third, and the fullest, edition appeared in 1987 when V. Bortnevskii edited the diary for the Leningrad University Press. This is the first English translation of this diary.

---

[1] Diary of 1812: № 49 (March 2), № 51 (March 5),. № 57 (March 9), № 59 (March 12), № 63 (March 16), № 65 (March 19), № 69 (March 23), № 71 (March 26), № 75 (March 30), № 78 (April 3); Diary of 1813: № 81 (April 6), № 83 (April 9), № 87 (April 13), № 88 (April 17), № 91 (April 20), № 93 (April 22), № 99 (April 30), № 105 (May 9), № 110 (May 14), № 113 (18 May); Diary of 1814 : № 115 (May 21), № 118 (25 May), № 120 (May 28), № 125 (June 4), № 129 (June 8), № 131 (11 June).

[2] *Otechestvennaya voina 1812 goda. Istoricheskie materialy leib-gvardii Semeyonovskogo Polka.* Poltava, 1912.

THE 1812 CAMPAIGN

Upon our departure from St. Petersburg, Colonel [Karl Antonovich] Kriedener commanded the Life Guard Semeyonovskii Regiment. Colonel [Fedor Nikolayevich] Posnikov commanded the 1st Battalion while Baron [Maxim Ivanovich] de-Damas (future Minister of Foreign Affairs of France during the reign of Louis XVIII)[3] was a commander of the 2nd Battalion. Colonel [Alexander Alexandrovich] Pisarev led the 3rd Battalion.

Since I served in the 3rd Battalion, I think it will be useful to list company commanders of this battalion: Captain [Sergei Alexandrovich] Kostomarov commanded the 3rd Grenadier Company; Captain [Gavrila Semenovich] Okunev – 7th Company; Captain [Christophor Alexandrovich] Brinken – 8th Company; Captain [Paul] Pushin – 9th Company.

MARCH

9 [21] March. Saturday

We had left St. Petersburg. I was the commander of the 9th Company which included 165 privates and 16 non-commissioned officers. Our company included the following officers: me, [Alexander] Chicherin, two Princes Trubetskoy (Sergey and Alexander) - Sergey was eventually exiled to Siberia for events of 14 December [1825],[4] while Chicherin was [seriously] wounded at Kulm [on 30 August 1813] and died several days later in Prague. In addition, two sub-ensigns were assigned to us: [Alexander Zakharovich] Zotov and Prince Dadiani. As soon as we reached Pulkovo, I found there my sisters with Mme B. and spent this last evening amidst my precious and dear family.

---

[3] Ange Hyacinthe Maxence, baron de Damas (1785-1862) was born into a French noble family, which fled the turmoil of the Revolution in the 1790s. He later enlisted in the Russian army, served in the Life Guard Semeyonovskii Regiment and later commanded the Astrakhanskii Grendier Regiment in 1812-1814, reaching the rank of major general. After the end of the Napoleonic Wars, he returned to France, where he served as the Minister of War in 1823-1824 and the Minister of Foreign Affairs in 1824-1828.

[4] Pushin refers to the Decembrist Uprising of 1825. Sergey Trubetskoy (1790-1860) was one of the leaders of the Northern Society and was court-martialed and sentences to 20 years of labor in Siberia.

10 [22] March. Sunday

Alarm woke us up very early in the morning. I bid farewell to my family and, greatly saddened by our separation, I began this march in low spirits. Strong wind was blowing. Our regimental headquarters stopped at Gatchina and my company marched another 10 *verstas* before halting at the village of Chernitsa.

11 [23] March. Monday

After departing from Chernitsa, I realized that I left my wallet there and, as soon as we halted at community of Rozhdestvenno, I sent [my people] to find it while I continued to work on correspondence with my relatives. My servant [*denshik*] returned towards evening and to my great pleasure he brought all my money back.

12 [24] March. Tuesday

Bivouac. I mailed my letters today

13 [25] March. Wednesday

It was very cold today. We departed at 8:00 a.m. and halted at Sorochkino. My main desire was to write my diary and letters home, but it was impossible to do this here since officers from the two other companies were billeted with us. We played cards and I won.

14 [26] March. Thursday

The regimental headquarters moved to Dolgovka, while my company advanced further ahead and stopped for the night some three *versta*s from the main road at the village Bolotye; officers of my company, as well those from another company, were billeted at the lodging house next to the road. The mistress of the houses wept incessantly, although everyone behaved very well towards her.

15 [27] March. Friday.

At 6:00 a.m. I, accompanied with a non-commissioned officer, went to see my company. This short walk was very unpleasant. It was cold morning and strong wind was blowing. Snow completely covered the road and we had fallen through snow on several occasion. After finally joining my soldiers, I marched with them to catch up with the regiment, which was gathering on the main road on which we marched to Luga; we arrived there in the afternoon. I suffered frostbite on my right ear. The regimental headquarters stopped at Luga. I also rested my company and used that time to run to the post, where, to my great joy, I found letters from home. After a bivouac, I marched with my company for about 10 *versta*s beyond Luga and stopped for the night at Rakovichi. It was a very tiring march.

16 [28] March. Saturday

A day of rest. I personally went to Luga to receive my [special] pay, which the Emperor had granted to us.[5]

17 [29] March. Sunday

The regimental headquarters moved to Gorodetz, and my company stopped at Yubra. As a duty officer, I remained at Gorodetz since I had to report [to my superiors] and reached Yubra and joined my company only in the evening

18 [30] March. Monday

We are in Zapolye. The peasant, in whose house we stopped, was a 130 years old man.

19 [31] March. Tuesday

We are in Veleni, to the right of the main road. Heavy snowfall complicated our advance.

20 March [1 April]. Wednesday

A day of rest. The house, where we were billeted, had a stove without a chimney so the smoke almost suffocated us. The owner of our house was an old man of some 135 years of age and he remembered Peter the Great and told us about his younger brother, who was 100 years old and who, he said, was still young.

21 March [2 April]. Thursday

---

[5] Pushin refers to a special payment, in the amount of one third of annual salary, issues to the troops of the Life Guard Semeyonovskii Regiments in order to facilitate their campaign preparations.

We are in Opoki, about two *versta*s from Borovichi, where our regimental headquarters is located. In the morning I reproached Chicherin for his discourteous attitude but later I was reprimanded by Colonel Kriedener, our regimental commander, who, as he passed our company, found, as usual, some things to criticize.

22 March [3 April]. Friday

We are in the town of Porkhov. Our brigade general Baron [Gregory Vladimirovich] Rosen passed us today and ordered us to rest troops tomorrow, although the rest was scheduled for the day after tomorrow. We certainly welcomed this order since it was incomparably more pleasant for us to stay in a town than in a village. For me personally, this rest was also important since I was concerned about my letters since Mme. B. informed me that her husband learned that she accompanied me to Pulkovo.

23 March [4 April]. Saturday

A day of rest.

24 March [5 April]. Sunday

We are at Kuznetsovo, while the regimental headquarters is at Golodushki. The land between Porkhovo and Kuznetsova is quite picturesque but a strong wind and bad weather made this march very unpleasant.

25 March [6 April]. Monday

At Lipovik, not far from the regimental headquarters which is at Sorokino. [Sub Lieutenant Nikolai] Kashkarev[6] caught up with us today and delivered several letters from Mme B. and several trinkets which she sent for me. Her letters touched me very much as she reproached me for not receiving any letters for over a month, which saddened me as well.

26 March [7 April]. Tuesday

---

[6] After the Napoleonic Wars ended, Kashkarev eventually commanded the 1st Grenadier Company and became known for starting the Life Guard Semeyonovskii Regiment's famed uprising in 1820, for which he was court-martialed, deprived of his awards and demoted to rank-and-file.

At Stega. As soon as we arrived here, I rented a peasant carriage to travel to the regimental headquarters at Ashevo. Being a duty officer for the regiment, I delivered my report to the regimental commander and took advantage of this opportunity to ask him for a furlough of several days to visit my estate which not far from our deployment. The colonel promised to satisfy my request.

27 March [8 April]. Wednesday

At my estate in Zhadritsy.[7] The regiment was supposed to gather at Sisino and, since the road from Stega was passing through the village of Ashevo, I asked Chicherin to remind Adjutant [Nikolai] Sipyagin to ask the colonel to approve my furlough. Everything was quickly resolved and Sipyagin gave me my furlough permit for five days. I immediately transferred the command of the company to Chicherin, rented a carriage and an hour later I was already in Novorzhev. I found here [Sub Lieutenant Fedor] Panyutin (who later distinguished himself during the Hungarian Campaign),[8] who was sent to gather bread for the regiment. We had a simple meal and talked for a long time about [Mikhail] Speransky and Mikhail Magnitsky, who were accused of treason.[9]

Following this meeting, I traveled to Zhadritsy, which was some 15 *versta*s away from Novorzhev, and found my uncle [Mikhail Pushin] already asleep. My uncle was an eccentric man. He was very glad to see me since his only solace was the society of a local priest [Ioan Fedoseev], whom he immediately called. The awkwardly arranged room, eccentric appearance of my uncle and the sycophancy of the priest, who tried to grab and kiss my hand – all of this stunned me at first. As I recovered, I went to the church to pay my respects to my father's grave.[10] I decided to

---

[7] The Pushin family estate of Zhadritsy was located about 25 *versts* away from Mikhailovskoye in the Novorzhervskii *uezd* (district) of the Pskov *gubernia* (province). The famous Russian poet Alexander Pushkin was exiled to Mikhailovskoye in the 1820s and Pushin established good relations with him.

[8] Pushin added this note years later and it refers to the Russian invasion of Hungary in 1849, when Emperor Nicholas I dispatched his troops to assist the Austrians in suppressing the Hungarian Revolt.

[9] Mikhail Speransky was Emperor Alexander's close advisor, who proposed a series of liberal reforms to modernize empire but faced increasing opposition and was disgraced and exiled in mid March 1812. Sparensky's dismissal effectively meant the end of liberal changes in Russia. Mikhail Magnitsky, Speransky's supporter, was also exiled, but later emerged as one of the leading reactionaries

[10] Pushin's father, Sergey Pushin, died in 1811.

stay in a small room with a fascinating view through its large Venetian window in a small house that my sister designed for me.

28 March [9 April]. Thursday

I woke up with a severe headache and suffered from a gas-poisoning. The Likhachevs – our neighbors and friends – invited me to visit them so I traveled with my uncle to them. Because of my uncle's mediocre costume, I hoped we would not meet anyone but I was disappointed to find M. Muromtsev, a first-rate dandy, at the Likhachev's estate. My godparents, despite all of this, welcomed me with open hands. I met them for the first time since my childhood. They were very pleasant people and we stayed with them until 4:00 p.m., before returning to Zhadritsy.

29 March [10 April]. Friday

Another neighbor, Neyelov, visited me and together we attended a mass.

30 March [11 April]. Saturday

I received the sacraments and immediately left the Zhadritsy estate to return to my company, which, marching to Grishino, was supposed to pass one of my estates. I met Chicherin and treated my soldiers to vodka. I spent the evening talking to my uncle about Speransky and Magnitsky.

31 March [12 April]. Sunday

Another mass – they are my uncle's true passion. The decree on the recruitment levy reached our village.[11] I was saddened by the thoughts about the dangers facing our dear Motherland.

APRIL

---

[11] Pushin refers to Emperor Alexander's manifesto of 23 March 1812 that required recruitment of 2 men per every 500 souls.

1 [13] April. Monday

Despite my uncle's superstition that it was a bad omen to start a trip on Monday, I attended the church with him, listened to a farewell mass, bid goodbye to my uncle and departed the village of Garkushino to visit the Likhachevs. [As I departed], the horses almost smashed me, which only further convinced my uncle that Monday was indeed a grave day. He bitterly cried as he bid farewell to me. Around 7:00 p.m. I finally reached Likhachevs, who welcomed my arrival and laid me into a feather bed [*pukhovaya postel*] in which I almost completely drowned; despite my protests that I was not accustomed to sleeping in such a soft bed, I had no choice but to do as I was told and, as a result, I slept very poorly that night.

2 [14] April. Tuesday

I woke up at 3:00 a.m. and, supplied with a vast number of provisions, reached the village of Bolgotovo by 6:00 a.m. Having changed my horses, I proceeded to the village of Opochka. Strong wind and snow on the road greatly delayed me. I found my regiment on a bivouac at Opochka, where it was awaiting the arrival of the Emperor [Alexander]. Here I received letters from which I learned that my letters had been delivered to their addressees in St. Petersburg. A large crowd of recruits stood in the street in front of my window. They sang joyous songs, while nearby their mothers and wives bitterly cried.

3 [15] April. Wednesday

At the village of Ryupigo. A day full of predicaments. The march was unbearably difficult because of constant anticipation that the Emperor would reach us at any moment, but in the end we had only seen his coach while the Emperor himself is expected tomorrow. One NCO from my company had lost his bayonet, while one soldier from the company train [rotnii oboz] stayed behind at Opochka, and was found only some time later. [Lieutenant Gavrila Gavrilovich] Bibikov, this repulsive man, joined us so our peaceful existence comes to an end. Chicherin entertained himself by tormenting Bibikov, but I was fed with all of this.

4 [16] April. Thursday

At Sebezh. We are in Byelorussian lands since yesterday. We slept late [today]. The regimental commander [Kriedener] noticed that our company wagon [rotnii furgon] passed too late and a soldier that accompanied it was not dressed as required; the Emperor was expected any moment now and he considered such disorder unpardonable so I was placed under arrest and released only after the regiment reached its bivouac. I was at least comported by the letters I received that day. M-me B. informed that she recovered from her illness and went out into the city. My cousin Nikolai [Pushin][12] also wrote me a few more details about her.

5 [17] April. Friday

Bivouac at Sebezh. Colonel Posnikov and other officers expressed their sympathy regarding my misadventure yesterday, which was very touching. Bibikov, despite all the abuse he was put through, spoke more than anyone else and was distraught that Colonel Kriedener treated me so severely.

6 [18] April. Saturday

At Trushuli, about 2 *versta*s from the regimental headquarters that is set up at the village of Lyakhovo. Spring is already in the air, but a heavy rain soaked us during the entire march. The territory we passed is truly amazing and if I were not soaked to the bone, I would have certainly observed it with much pleasure. We bivouacked in an open field, which is not very pleasant during a heavy rain. At Trushuli, I was given a ghastly room, full of various insects and without flooring, but I still could not enjoy it since I was a duty officer for the regiment and, without any available carriage, I had to travel on horse with a report to Lyakhovo. My meeting with the regimental commander proved to be cold, it seemed he sought to avoid explaining [his actions] and I tried to free myself from him as soon as I could. I informed Colonel Posnikov, our battalion commander, that I take off responsibility for the precision of the movement of the company train with other regimental trains; Colonel Kriedener canceled his earlier order and announced that he was not

[12] In 1812, Nikolai Nikolayevich Pushin served as an ensign in the Life Guard Litovskii [Lithuanian] Regiment. After the Napoleonic Wars, he became a member in secret societies and became close to the future Decembrists, including A. Pestel. In 1822, he publicly confronted Grand Duke Constantine for abusive treatment of officers of the Life Guard Litovskii Regiment, for which he was court martialed and sentenced to death, which was later commuted to reduction in ranks and loss of nobility and all awards. Despite such harsh punishment, Pushin stoically endured his hardships as a private in the regiment, refusing offers from his former comrades to continue living in officer quarters. In late 1823, he was restored in the rank of 1823, and after five years of exemplary service, he was promoted to a colonel. By 1834, his past misdeed was forgotten and he was appointed to lead the Noble Regiment, promoted to a major general in 1836 and to lieutenant general in 1847.

insisting on having all 12 wagons moving together, and instead was allowing company commanders to act on their own discretion when deciding the time of dispatch for each of their company wagons. Therefore, my arrest had produced some positive results since it affected the order beneficially for all my friends, and I was fully satisfied with this.

7 [19] April. Sunday

At the village of Kashirino. The lands we passed are frightfully deprived. The road is full of the poor and blind. The local landowners are to be blamed for this misery but I wonder who is responsible for such high number of the blind. The *rentiers* [*arendator*], desiring to gain as much profit as possible, burden the peasants with such heavy *corvee* that the latter had no time left to work for themselves. I was told this by a peasant belonging to a certain Shadulskii, who loaned his peasants to a Russian merchant. The populace living in this region is also prone for indolence. Today, Prince Dadiani, who is constantly grumbling, moaning and complaining about the hardships of the campaign, suddenly gathered courage and decided to jump across a stream, but miscalculated and instead of landing on the opposite bank, he found himself up to his neck in the water. I let an NCO to help him, but, to complete the prince's misery, the regimental commander passed by and, upon seeing the laughable figure of Prince Dadiani, he got furious and punished Prince Dadiani by ordering him to serve as a private for the rest of the campaign.

8 [20] April. Monday

At the village of Shavelki. The regimental headquarters at Rositsy. The area is indeed wonderful. Passing through Rositsy, stopped for a few minutes to warm myself and saw my company pass by me, with none of platoons [*vzvod*] falling behind each other. Chicherin took advantage of my absence and ordered a rest. I was displeased with Chicherin acting without my knowledge, immediately ordered the company to continue marching, and then reprimanded Chicherin, who, in turn, responded with impudence and told me that he refuses to share quarters with my anymore. I eagerly agreed with him and told him that he would now be quartered with Bibikov, whom he could not bear. The very idea of putting them together appealed to me and, although our conversation soon became friendly, I made a firm decision to remove Chicherin from our quarters. He began to tease Bibikov and, as a joke, he told him that although they would share quarters, they would need to eat separately.

9 [21] April. Tuesday

The order to halt at Shavelky disappointed us since we had poor quarters there. This was caused by the leading column that got hold up at Druya and could not cross the Dvina River due to the floating ice.

10 [22] April. Wednesday

At the village of Druya. The march was quite pleasant, and weather was wonderful. Until now, the weather was quite bad which only complicated the marching; we still could not get accustomed to such changing weather. Our battalion had difficulties in crossing the Dvina because the ice began to float again. I had a minor argument with Sipyagin, with whom I shared a breakfast during the crossing. We received the order to set up quarters and to not march to Vilna. Druya itself is located in a beautiful area.

11 [23] April. Thursday

Bivouac at Druya. A torrential rain kept pouring and the resulting mud prevented us from getting out for the entire day. A Jew named Movsha carried out all of our instructions, received three rubles and left quite satisfied and happy.

12 [24] April. Friday

At the village of Salki. Prior to our departure from Druya, our regimental commander gathered us on the bank of the Dvina to meet the Emperor, who, according to him, was expected any minute. The heavy rain had no mercy on us and, to complete our misery, a feld-jager delivered the news that his Majesty, whom we were awaiting for so long, had not yet left the Tsarskoye Selo.[13] So we returned to our quarters without any results to show except for getting soaked to our bones so that we did not break this habit. [Later that day] an alarm call was not heard in my company, which was located at the end of the village, and I was unpleasantly surprised upon being told that the entire regiment was assembled for an hour and was delayed by my company alone. We rushed at once but Colonel Kriedener, naturally, did not miss this opportunity to reprimand me. The regimental headquarters moved to the village of Ikazni, while my company, upon approaching this village, turned left and occupied nine nearby settlements; I stopped at Salki, and my host was a

---

[13] Alexander departed from St. Petersburg on 21 April and reached Vilna on 26 April.

14

small *rentier* by the name of Salmanovich, an 80-year old man, with two daughters, one of whom is not so bad looking.

13 [25] April. Saturday

Chicherin spent the night with us but this morning he was assigned to new quarters in another village, so he moved there.

14 [26] April. Sunday

All captains (company commanders) were ordered to arrive to the regiment commander at Ikazn' at 10:00 a.m. I was among those who arrived. We were ordered to gather most detailed information on the amount of supplies that can be obtained in the villages occupied by our troops. The reports were supposed to specify precisely how much grain, forage and cattle, belonging either to peasant communities or to landowners, was available. The poles were quite bewildered by this order. I was very disappointed to cause so many problems to the poor Salmanovich, who had very few belongings and he proved to be a very good man.

15 [27] April. Monday

The Emperor had traveled through Druya three days ago. Bibikov arrived this evening and, as an ill-omened bird, he brought the news that officers were prohibited from using carriages anymore.

16 [28] April. Tuesday

One of our officers, [Nikolai Nikolayevich] Khrushev arrived tonight. He traveled for provisions to Druya and took a NCO from my company as an escort.

17 [29] April. Wednesday

I received an order to obtain from my host a declaration (notice) listing his entire property. The declaration form was sent from the regiment. This news anguished the entire Salmanovich family. Bibikov was right and we were allowed to keep only transport horses, not even the riding horses. I did not dare to leave my village. Meantime, orders were rapidly changing one after another. I ordered Zotov to deliver my letter to the post office in Druya. He traveled with A. Trubetskoy and his brother

Sergei also departed, leaving me alone; to be precise, almost alone since Prince Dadiani also stayed at home. He is a simpleton [*prostofilya*] who either sleeps or sits mum. Tonight he suddenly jumped up after being frightened by a small dog, which had unnoticeably crawled under his bed, and began shouting at full strength, swearing that he felt as the devil himself strolled over him.

19 April [1 May] Friday

This morning all company quartermasters were ordered to arrive to Ikazn'. We were guessing reasons for the entire day before learning from an order, which was received in the evening that three companies, including mine, had to change their quarters in the morning. This removed us further from Druya, which was not particularly pleasing for me since I began to court one of Salmanovich's daughters; they were indeed very good people.

20 April [2 May]. Saturday

At Ukla, at a local estate. This was the first march that I made on foot. We arrived at Ukla around noon. Local *rentier* is a certain Rodzevich. It seems that he is richer than our Salmanovich, but, despite his courteousness, we still noticed certain hostility which the Poles often demonstrate towards the Russians. This was enough for us to regret leaving our old quarters. [At Ukla] we found the Izmailovtsy [troops from the Life Guard Izmailovskii Regiment] who had previously occupied our new quarters, so we had to share quarters awaiting their departure. These minor troubles were eclipsed by the joy brought to me by the letters of M-me B. that I received here. She has not written to me in a long time.

21 April [3 May]. Sunday

It is Easter. On such days the Poles only eat. Table is constantly set but the locals sit around on usual time only to eat some soup. I traveled to Colonel Pisarev, who was entertaining a female society. We learned that the day after tomorrow we are departing for Komai, a village located near Svencionys, close to Vilna.

22 April [4 May]. Monday

I again traveled to Colonel Pisarev. They arranged dances tonight.

23 April [5 May]. Tuesday

At Oksyutovichi. The regimental headquarters is at Zamoshye. Despite the permission for captains to ride their horses, I decided not to use this right and marched on foot the entire march of 24 *versta*s. After reaching Zamoshye, we turned right. Bidding farewell to Rodzevich was not as touching as with Salmanovich. The residents of Oksyutovichi are all Russians.

24 April [6 May]. Wednesday

We unexpectedly received order to halt. We assumed that this was due to the lack of supplies. Our soldiers have received their rations for two days and are now busy preparing bread. The Russians living at Oksyutovichi are not serfs but rather free men but they cannot leave their land and are considered *chinsheviki*.[14] They are not subject to *barshina* [labor service] but instead pay some forty rubles for land to their landlord Muruzi. This essentially equals to serfdom. After lunch we travelled to visit our friends billeted in nearby villages. We got such a poor peasant horse that we got more tired riding it that we would have been if chose to walk. We forgot to procure some candles and am now writing with great difficulty under a dim light of candle-end.

25 April [7 May]. Thursday.

At Bogin'ki. The regiment's headquarters is at Ugor. We moved about eight *versta*[15] away from the headquarters. The road ran in the lovely woods bordering the lake, around which our village was located. We had to walk around the lake to get to the village. It is so unpleasant to be able to your quarters and yet be unable to get there at once. I sent my [servant] Lukyan [Prokofiev] to Vidzy, a small town about two *versta*s from Boginki. He returned quite late, brought some items but no letters.

26 April [8 May]. Friday.

At Babyany. Snow and wind greatly hindered our progress. We crossed the Dvina River across a rather meager pontoon bridge. During the crossing of the 3rd Company, the bridge was shaking, so I halted my

---

[14] *Chinsheviki* were free peasants in Lithuania and western Byelorussia who were perpetual renters of landlords' lands for which they paid a special tax, known as *chinsh*, which was abolished in 1860s.

[15] One *versta* is equal to 1.06 km.

company and did not allow it to pass in closed column, but instead moved it in open order, by platoons, at intervals, and only thanks to this [method] we were able to safely cross to the opposite shore. Immediately upon arrival in Babyany I went with a report to Tverech, a small town, which our regimental headquarters was set up; I was on duty. I did not find our regimental commander, who dined at [Captain 2nd class Ivan] Kartsev's house, so I did not wait for his return. This trip, however, did not go in vain, because I learned that there were letters received on my name, delivered by some soldier whom I could not find. Nevertheless, I calmed down since receiving letters meant that everyone back at home was fine.

27 April [9 May]. Saturday.

[We are] at the village of Butsevichi, about four *versta*s from the regimental headquarters set up at Komai. This is the site of our new quarters. Our march here was very tiring and unpleasant due to bad weather. We are located in dreadful place, the village is so poor that virtually nothing can be procured here. And there is no forage here.

28 April [10 May]. Sunday.

In the morning I visited Colonel Pisarev. He was preoccupied with relocating his quarters and was moving into the house of a certain landowner Kholmskii. I bid farewell to him and returned to dine in Butsevichi. In the evening we learnt that the Grand Duke [Constantine] has scheduled a review for our unit.

29 April [11 May]. Monday.

The next morning I again went on horseback to Pisarev to discuss the forthcoming review, but did not find him at home and stayed for dinner at Kholmskii's house. I then returned back with [Lieutenant Pavel] Khrapovitskii, who told me that all company commanders were required to be at Komai by 5 o'clock. Concerned that I will be late, I rushed home, put on a scarf and went at once to Komai. Arriving there I discovered that there was an error – the order concerned only battalion commanders, but I exploited this opportunity to ask for permission to change my billet, which I received. My entire company searched the area around Butsevichi for appropriate quarters. First we went to Dvorochany. The house there was so dirty that we did not dare to occupy it. Alexander Trubetskoy and I then walked for two *versta*s to Zagach to inspect another house, which, although uninhabited, had some advantage over others. It was already dusk when we returned to Dvorochany to inform our comrades of our discovery, and our servants had not yet arrived. The wife of a tenant in Dvorochany impatiently waited for our departure, and she suffered as much as we because of this delay. Her husband treated us, fully sharing his better half's sentiments. This affair continued well into the night until everyone gathered and only then we went to Zagach. But, oh Lord, how badly we suffered here – there were no glass in the windows, no chairs, no table.

30 April [12 May]. Tuesday.

Because of yesterday's fatigue, I slept soundly. But this morning we realized that we have settled in the worst place possible. So again Alexander Trubetskoy and I went in search of a neighboring nobleman, but his home was rather poverty-stricken. He had ten children and there were five of us, so he could not accommodate us. The poor lad was very concerned that we would decided to stay at his house and solemnly promised to deliver everything we might need at Zagach. He did keep his word, and, thus, we finally settled down. Yesterday, at Komai, I saw a church built Gediminas[16] [some] 397 years ago. Its brick walls are of extraordinary thickness. One is also drawn to a chapel, built by Countess Silistrowskii some 40 years ago. The icon of St. John and the portrait of Gediminas have been preserved from the very foundation of the church. But the icon is in better shape than portrait. The dungeon is used as family sepulcher for the genus of Count Silistrowski, and one can even see bones of the dead.

MAY

1 [13] May. Wednesday.

Delightful weather. I spent the whole day walking. The area is picturesque. We can observe Postavy – a village on the other side of the lake.

2 [14] May. Thursday.

---

[16] Gediminas (d. 1341) was the Grand Duke of Lithuania, who conducted several campaigns against the Russian principalities that were weakened by the Mongol invasion. The church was probably laid by the Gediminas but completed around 1415 (1812 minus 397 years) after his death, otherwise Pushin is wrong in referring to him.

I reviewed each platoon of my company; they were deployed in the villages of Dashki, Drabeshi, Matsuty and Butsevichi. Chicherin was at Matsuty and I stopped by to see him for a minute. In Butsevichi I was very displeased to find everything in disorder. I then went to Pisarev, but he was not at home. I stayed to dine with the officers of the 8th Company, who were quartered with him, and waited for his return. Review was scheduled for the next day and I needed to talk to him. Excessive pedantry disappointed me, but back home I found a very happy man - Prince Dadiani. His servant, beloved Basil, had arrived, and he hurried from far away to tell me about it.

3 [15] May. Friday.

Rats prevented us from sleeping throughout the night. I got up at 5 o'clock, and soon arrived with my company to Komai, where our commander Kriedener was supposed to review us. He was very critical of me, so I returned to Zagach in a very bad mood.

5 [17] May. Sunday.

The Trubetskoys went to Svencionys, while I got to Postavy. The village has a school for 100 pupils, there is a main square surrounded by shops. There was not much trading going on, but the school master told me that there will be a fair on the 9th and I would then see how everything comes to life. He invited me to dine with him that day. I returned home to dine and a little later received orders to depart at night. We still had one more review.

6 [18] May. Monday.

At Lukashevschizna. I departed at 2 am and stopped at rather cramped quarters at 9 o'clock.

8 [20] May. Wednesday.

I was on duty and, as I was going with the report [to the headquarters], I learned that the Grand Duke had not yet given us any definite order regarding the review, and that our commander had moved in order to be ready when the order is issued. For the third day already our situation is turning from bad to worse, and we are deprived of everything.

9 [21] May. Thursday.

At Matskovichi, in landowner's house. We were given slightly better quarters not far from the town Lyntuny, where the Grand Duke was supposed to review us. The regiment's headquarters remained at Komai. Departing from Lukashevschizna, I noticed that I had a deserter. This made me very upset.[17] At Matskovichi, the local tenant was a certain Buinevich, his sister would not be a bad one, if not for her red hair.

10 [22] May. Friday.

I slept badly today. The weather was terrible and I was not feeling well.

11 [23] May. Saturday.

Chekhovich, the owner of the village Matskovichi, paid me a visit. I received a letter from M-me. B. and sent Luka to Svencionys to take my letter to the post. I do not know where the [Life Guard] Lithuanian Regiment is deployed, so I am unable to see with my cousin, Nicholas, whom I have not seen since leaving St. Petersburg.

12 [24] May. Sunday.

Bibikov arrived to spend evening with us and stayed the night, which was beyond our expectations. He is extremely annoying.

13 [25] May. Monday.

The letter I received today from M-me. B. calmed me down and put me in a good mood, so distressed by Bibikov's presence. [We] received order to move once again to Lukashevschizna tomorrow. There will be maneuvers held in the presence of the Grand Duke at Lyntuny on May 15 [27].

14 [26] May. Tuesday.

At Lukashevschizna. The march here was not difficult but very unpleasant because of bad weather. We departed at 4:00 am in strong winds and snow. Our quarters are not very comfortable.

---

[17] Private Tit Gavrilov left the regiment but returned on 26 May.

15 [27] May. Wednesday.

At 5 o'clock we went to Lyntuny. By the arrival of the Grand Duke, we made through the woods and deployed on the plain between the forest and village. The exercises were very successful, the Grand Duke was very pleased, and he personally told me so. I would have liked less praise but more rest. It is doggone cold [*sobachii kholod*]. After the maneuvers I returned with my company to Lukashevschizna, fed my soldiers there, and then went back to Matskovichi.

16 [28] May. Thursday.

Due to the high costs of tea, our company decided to forsake it. I took up the construction of barracks in our huge yard.

17 [29] May. Friday.

Prince Alexander Trubetskoy and I visited Pisarev, who was in Korodino, the estate of Count Silistrowski. Along the way, passing through Komai, we met Colonel Kriedener who, this time, treated us very kindly. The road from Komai to Korodino is wonderful as it runs through a birch forest. Komai itself is located on a hill, and therefore it is perfectly visible. Officers of the 3rd Grenadier Company settled together with Colonel Pisarev, and we all had a very pleasant dinner. Even reclusive Colonel Kriedener came to us, but as the darkness approached we had to think about returning to Matskovichi.

19 [31] May. Sunday.

Weather had improved slightly. I went to Komai. As I approached it, the procession was already emerging from the church so I stopped by [Lieutenant Ivan] Zhadovskii. He took me into the catacombs that were under the court house. Brick arches. In the vaults there are occasional holes that, however, pass too little light in order to be able to dispense with torches and move around without a guide. They say that these caves once served as a prison. By lunchtime, I returned home. One of my horses struck the driver in the head, but, fortunately, nothing dangerous, just a slight injury.

20 May [1 June]. Monday.

Chicherin came to me to announce that he had asked Colonel Kriedener to put me to his billet. According to him, [Prince Lieutenant Alexander] Golitsyn, who shared a billet with him, had insulted him. Golitsyn, in turn, also came to me and explained that they quarreled over a net, which he asked Chicherin to take to have some fun fishing in a lake.

21 May [2 June]. Tuesday.

In the evening we learned that in two days we are going to Vilna, where we will stay for a few days.

22 May [3 June]. Wednesday.

My barracks is completed, and Pisarev, visited me for breakfast. Yesterday and today I received letters from my sisters and M-me. B. They all sent me various interesting trinkets. I was very touched by their attention. To my great joy my cousin Nicholas visited me in the evening. The thought of tomorrow's march greatly depressed me. Fortunately, Konstantinovo, where we marched, was just one *versta* away from the Svir, where my brother Nicholas was stations, so he stayed with us until morning.

23 May [4 June]. Thursday.

At Kutski, a village one *versta* away from Konstantinovo, where the regimental headquarters is set up. Nicholas walked with us for the entire march and then stayed with us all night, as his regiment is departing only on Sunday. Our battalion was on march since 5 am and stopped at common quarters in the village of Kutski. Colonel Kriedener's billet is also there. As I was entering the village with my company, he was in the street and treated me kindly, which is probably no accident.

24 May [5 June]. Friday.

At Babichi. Not far from the town of Mikhalishki where the regimental headquarters is. The battalion departed at 4 am. I parted with Nicholas in the hope that we shall see each other in Vilna. Three companies of the 1st Battalion suddenly came across our battalion on march, and, to my great delight, I saw Panyutin. We were comrades in

Petersburg, and had not met in fifteen days since departing the city. Today we got to the main road from Svencionys to Vilna. Passed through the village of Strachy, if I am not mistaken; the road descends to the dam and turns sharply to the left. Location is picturesque. There is a lovely stream on the left, and a steep cliff, covered with magnificent forest, on the right. The sun was rising just as when we reached this wonderful place, and added even more splendor to this landscape. From the dam to our quarters the road run through the woods. The battalion stopped not far from Mikhalishki because we could not cross the Viliya which flows in front of that village.

25 and 26 May [6-7 June]. Saturday and Sunday.

At 1:00 am we left Babichi, crossed the Viliya on the dam, passed through Mikhalishki and walked until halting at Vorony. About two *versta*s farther our quarters were already prepared and reached them only by 5 o'clock in the morning. We stayed here until the evening and departed before the sunset. At first marching was quite nice, soldiers sang, the weather was wonderful, the road was straightforward, but, as night fell and we all became drowsy, the situation changed. Despite the fact that I smoked a pipe and kept building air castles, I could not get used to the idea that I was not in bed. On a halt, next to some tavern, where we had a quick snack, I fell asleep so soundly that I did not hear the drums beating, caused some displeasure in Colonel Pisarev. At 5 am we stopped in the village Gaiduny, about two *versta*s from Vilna.

27 May [8 June]. Monday.

A day of rest [*dnevka*] at Gaiduny [Gaidūnai]. The soldiers are busy preparing for the entry into Vilna. The commander came to see me and we discussed family quarrel between our guests, when the Prince [George] of Oldenburg[18] passed through the village, so I chose not to show myself to His Highness, who left as soon as he arrived. [The Life Guard] Finland Regiment is quartered with us.

28 May [9 June]. Tuesday.

We were kept under arms since 2 a.m., even approached the gates of Vilna, but after a long delay, we were ordered not to enter the city and

---

[18] Prince George of Oldenburg was married to Grand Duchess Catherine, the sister of Emperor Alexander I. He served as the head of communications and governor of the Tver, Yaroslavl and Novgorod provinces.

instead take quarters in the suburbs and around the city. The Emperor did not see us. For the night we went to Gury [Guriai], an ugly village some three *versta*s from Vilna. I slept under an open sky because there were too many of us in a rather squalid room.

29 May [10 June]. Wednesday.

We were under arms [again] since 3 a.m. It was cold weather. We walked through the city, and our whole division was drawn up in battle array at Pogulianka. We marched on a parade in front of the Emperor, who was very pleased with us. The review was over at 11 a.m.; we were placed in quarters inside the city - namely, in the suburb of Zarechye. Today, we are allowed ourselves some luxury. I dined with Nicholas in a tavern. The evening was spent in the opera, though a very bad one. They staged a performance of [Austrian composer Wenzel Müller's] "Sisters from Prague" [*Die Schwestern von Prag*].

30 May [11 June]. Thursday.

I tramped the pavement all day long. I paid a visit to [Colonel Nicholas] Selyavin, who promised to send my letters with the next courier.

31 May [12 June]. Friday.

Conducted training in the valley of Pogulianka. Some twenty three battalions, not counting artillery, were under arms. We left at 4 am and returned at 1 pm. Selyavin took my letters.

JUNE

1 [13] June. Saturday.

At Skaisteri. I really wanted to sleep a bit longer today, but the order forced us to get up at 6 o'clock in the morning. This disclosure was not particularly pleasant. Hoping to remain in Vilna a bit longer, we had not bothered to get a few necessary items that are so easy to get in this town but cannot be found in the untoward villages. In any case we had to part with the charms of this city. Fortunately, Skaysteri is just two *versta*s away from this comfortable city.

3 [15] June. Monday.

Before heading to Vilna, I went to the regimental headquarters that was set up in Wirzbah [?] for a leave pass. Upon entering the city, in front of the city hall, I met the head of the division General [Alexey] Ermolov, who instructed me to tell to commander Kriedener that we were leaving tomorrow. This wicked order had poisoned all of my enjoyment and compelled me to go to Kocherishki, about two *versta*s from Vilna. I arrived there at 7 pm, left the carriage on the main road and hurried to see Colonel Kridneru. He had just gone to [Staff Captain Alexander] Bernikov's company - I followed him there but again missed him by a few minutes. He borrowed a horse from Bernikov and finally found the colonel with [Colonel Vladimir von] Patkul. Having accomplished my order, I got on a horse to return to Bernikova, but got lost and found my way only 2 hours later. Finally, after all these adventures, I got onto the main road where the carriage still awaited me and returned to Skaisteri.

5 [17] June. Wednesday.

At Yazov, near Lovarishki. We left at 10 am. The heat was unbearable and the road sandy. My company passed through Lovarishki where regimental headquarters was established.

6 [18] June. Thursday.

At Lyadzino. We left at 5 pm. The battalion gathered at Zhebino, where we got on the main road not far from the inn, near which we slept during the night of 25-26 May. We were completely socked because of the heavy rain. After passing Vorony, we turned to the left and spent the night with 2nd Battalion at Lyadzino.

7 [19] June. Friday.

At Mikhalishki. The march was brief, only two *versta*s. We departed at 5 o'clock in very hot weather. The whole regiment halted at Mikhalishki.

8 [20] June. Saturday.

A day of rest at Mikhalishki. We went to see the village church, which is about 200 years old. In the cavern - a few tombs, in one of them we found a very well-preserved corpse of a priest. In other tombs there were only bones and a few hairs. In the evening the [Life Guard] Lithuanian

Regiment passed through Mikhalishki, and I managed to see my brother Nicholas.

9 [21] June. Sunday.

At Nareishi. We departed by companies at 3 o'clock in the morning. We crossed the Wiliya. My company stopped before the regimental headquarters. We were all bewildered by the appearance of a village girl, who quickly bowed to everyone in the legs. We were very befuddled and initially did not understand it, but soon it all became clear - she was a bride and, under local customs, she had to bow everyone in the legs. Soldiers were also amazed by this custom.

10 [22] June. Monday.

At Matskovichi. We departed by companies at midnight. The regimental headquarters stopped at Sarenchany, while my company took its old quarters. I reached Matskovichi when everyone was still asleep. The old landlady Buynovich was very happy to see me again and kept repeating, "Our dear captain returned."

11 [23] June. Tuesday.

At Myskova-on-Disna. I did nothing the whole day, just swimming in the Komai Lake.

12 [24] June. Wednesday.

I went to see Colonel Pisarev, who stopped at Chekhovich. There were M-mes. Mirskii, who charmed me with their kindness.

13 [25] June. Thursday.

I spent part of the day in the 8th company, talking about the upcoming campaign.

14 [26] June. Friday.

About 8 pm, as I was spending a pleasant time with M-mes. Mirskii, we received an order to depart by companies at once and make a forced march in Lyntuny. I hurried to Matskovichi and immediately marched with my company. After the midnight, we arrived and encamped at Lyntuny.

15 [27] June. Saturday.

Our brigade arrived an hour after me to Lyntuny, from where we marched to Svencionys and stopped about 8 *versta*s from that town. The French crossed the Niemen and are moving to Vilna. At 1 p.m. we moved to Svencionys, waited for the arrival of the Emperor, and after parading in front of him, we bypassed the town and stopped for rest on the road to Vilna that will lead us to the Glory.

16 [28] June. Sunday.

Our entire corps has concentrated. Grand Duke Constantine Pavlovich is charged with commanding the corps, which comprises of the entire Imperial Guard, that is, one division of infantry and one cavalry division. The head of our division - General Ermolov. Rumors claim that the French are already at Vilna.[19] I am again with my brother Nicholas, and recently met [Ensign of LG Izmailovskii Regiment Peter] Semenov whom I have not seen since leaving St. Petersburg.

17 [29] June. Monday.

Standing still. Rumours have it that there was a rearguard action near Vilna.[20].

18 [30] June. Tuesday.

March from Svencionys to the camps near Davgelishki. We departed at 4 o'clock in the morning. A heavy rain was falling. The road was difficult, and we marched for 11 hours straight. Forty people fell ill and one died in [our] regiment.

19 June [1 July]. Wednesday.

Standing still. Fortunately, rain fell intermittently during the day so we were able to somewhat dry out our clothes. Our commander, Colonel

---

[19] The French occupied Vilna on 28 June.

[20] Pushin probably refers to the actions at Antokol, one of Vilna's suburbs, involving the rearguard of the 3rd Infantry Corps

Kriedener, was livid, caused us a lot of trouble, arresting several officers for complete trifles. A certain Count Segur, a Frenchman and the first prisoner of war, was brought to our camp today.

20 June [2 July]. Thursday.

In camps between the Disna and Widza Rivers. Our corps marched at 4:30 a.m. As we departed my sergeant informed me that three soldiers of Polish descent have deserted.[21] With such a commander as ours, this was doubly upsetting for me: besides the fact that I personally did not like desertion, I now had had to expect plenty of criticism from this boorish person who has not missed a day to annoy any one of us. Today he had Prince Golitsyn arrested, which was completely unwarranted. Crossing the Disna, we approached the Widza. According to reports we had received, the French are advancing in three columns, of which one is moving against our right flank through Vilkomir.

21 June [3 July]. Friday.

Standing still. We heard several gun volleys in the rearguard. We do not know where a French corps, which we expected to meet at Svencionys, is moving to.

22 June [4 July]. Saturday.

At camps across the Widza. The corps of [Nikolai] Tuchkov [3rd Infantry Corps] and [Fedor] Uvarov [1st Cavalry Corps] departed at 6 a.m. and when they had passed us around 11 o'clock, we were also ordered to depart and follow them. We crossed the Widza, where the emperor himself came to see us. After moving through the town, we turned to the right-side route and stopped some two *versta*s from town. The march was only 15 *versta*s long but extreme heat exhausted us.

23 June [5 July]. Sunday.

Camp at Zamoshye. Our corps marched at 2 a.m. and covered 40 *versta*s in 15 hours. The heat was even stronger than yesterday, and despite three halts, our men were completely exhausted from fatigue. This march can compete with the Davgelishki march [for being the hardest one we made].

---

[21] These soldiers were Benedict Drabulis, Nikodim Jankowski and Jakub Baltyngose

24 June [6 July]. Monday.

Camp at Ikazn'. Our corps marched at 7 pm. It was quite dark when we pitched bivouacs. There was no fire, no wood for cooking, which was very uncomfortable after the thunderstorm that caught us en route.

25 June [7 July]. Tuesday.

Camp at Milashevo, on the road from the Disna to Druya. I was on duty and had a plenty of things to attend to on the road. Our corps departed at 3 p.m. and arrived quite early at Milashevo. This march can be considered only a stroll. The weather was wonderful, so our stay at the camp is quite enjoyable. At first we were told to get ready again for action, but then, to our delight, the order was canceled.

26 and 27 June [8-9 July]. Wednesday and Thursday.

Village of Leonpol and fortified positions at Drissa. We departed Milashevo at 3 pm and, after a 12-hour marching, arrived in Leonpol at 3 a.m. on the 27th. After staying here until 3 p.m., we moved towards Drissa, where our fortified positions are located. Our Sovereign let us pass by him as we were deploying in battle columns, and stared at us with a smile on his face, but I think his heart was burdened with other feelings. The enemy is between our army and the army of Prince Bagration.

28 June [10 July]. Friday.

Standing still. All corps of the 1st Western Army have concentrated at Drissa. Our corps - 5th. The army of Prince Bagration - 2nd Western Army, it is smaller in size than ours. From the order of the day we learned that there was a rearguard skirmish on the Vistula River, in which our troops have taken advantage.[22]

29 June [11 July]. Saturday.

Standing still. The guests dept coming to my little shed. We celebrated my birthday in the evening.

---

[22] Editor; Pushin is clearly mistaken since no rearguard actions could have taken place on the Vistula. It is possible that he refers to a combat near the village of Kocherishki fought on 6 July.

30 June [12 July]. Sunday.

Standing still.

JULY

1 [13] July. Monday.

In the morning, my company was assigned to bake bread, but a little later, this order was canceled, and each company dispatched four bakers instead. We received the news that the army of Prince Bagration had a dazzling fight at Mir.[23]

2 [14] July. Tuesday.

A bivouac on the road to Polotsk. At night, we received an order to be ready to march at once, but despite such an order, we departed at 8 am only. We crossed the Dvina river, covered about 11 *versta*s along its right bank to get to the road to Polotsk and be ready tp proceed at any moment.

3 [15] July. Wednesday.

Standing still. We were informed that [Jacob] Kulnev's advance guard successfully operated near Druya.[24] Order was issued to be ready to depart four minutes after the signal (three strokes of stick). The order was made after lunch. But this time it was a false alarm and we stayed in place.

4 [16]July. Thursday.

---

[23] Pushin refers to the actions at Mir where Ataman Matvei Platov defeated a Polish light cavalry brigade.

[24] On 14 July, Kulnev crossed the Dvina near Druya and made a sudden attack on the enemy cavalry, capturing some 100 men, including first enemy general.

Camp at Knyazhitsy. We departed at 2 o'clock, crossed the Drissa River and, after marching for another nine *versta*s in the direction of Polotsk, we pitched our bivouacs. Due to bad road, we reached our destination only at 9 pm.

5 [17] July. Friday.

Camp at Sokolitsy. We marched from 12 pm to 9 pm before halting with the 2nd Corps. Since the 29th [of June, 11 July], we are allowed to have only two pack horses per company. Today one of our horses got lost and was found – to everyone's joy - only at night.

6 [18] and 7 [19] July. Saturday and Sunday.

Camp at Polotsk. We left Sokolitsy at 3 o'clock in the afternoon, marched all night, and reached Polotsk at 7 am. It rained all night long, so the marching proved to be very tiring; yet we still had to make three more marches like that to forestall the French to Vitebsk. We held a thanksgiving service to mark [Ataman Matvei] Platov's victory at Mir. According to the reports, three French cavalry regiments were routed in this battle. The Emperor left the army for Moscow. One gunner, who wanted to serve in the cavalry, had deserted and joined one of our uhlan regiments; yet he was caught because of his hair cut and he was tried in Vilna. He was then taken prisoner after the enemy occupied the town but this brave fellow, although he was facing a death penalty at home, chose to escape from captivity, came to General Ermolov, and frankly told him everything. For such dedication, he was pardoned and enlisted in the cavalry regiment, as he desired.

8 [20] July. Monday.

Camp near the village of Oboli at Zuya. We departed at 1 am and after covering 35 *versta*s in 19 hours, we stopped near Obol, in a general direction to Vitebsk. As a duty officer, I had virtually no rest today. The regimental commander, Colonel Kriedener, in his usual habit of being rude, spoke impertinently with an officer from our battalion, a certain Khrapovitskii. (He told him: "You are walking like a doll in front of your platoon"). Wishing to teach the commander a lesson, all officers of the battalion decided to go and announce to him that in the future he could present all sorts of stern demands, but he should never dare to speak presumptuously to any officer. Our battalion commander, Colonel

Pisarev, learning about our intention, asked us not to go all at once, but rather let him talk to the regimental commander first. We accepted his offer and, as soon as we stopped for a bivouac, Colonel Pisarev went to Colonel Kriedener to convey all that we had told him. Colonel Kriedener was livid. He did not want to see all battalion officers, and instead demanded to meet only four company commanders: Kostomarov, Brinken, Okunev and me (Pushin). He did not allow us to utter a word and exhausted all possible threats against us, telling us he was struck by our inability to control our officers. To this we objected that the same can be said about him. In conclusion, he declared that he was giving us 24 hours to think and after this period he would expect a definite answer from us, on the basis of which he would then act. As we exited the commander's tent, we were met by all the officers of the regiment, who, upon hearing about the results of our negotiations, declared that, in 24 hours, they would also show up and repeat to the regimental commander everything that Colonel Pisarev had told him in the morning. In such a frame of mind, we all went to sleep.

9 [21] July. Tuesday.

Camp between Zenkovo and Zarechye. Continuing our advance to Vitebsk, our corps departed at 4 o'clock in the morning, marched for 25 *versta*s and stopped not far from Zarechye at 7 o'clock in the evening. In the morning Colonel Kriedener severely reprimanded me without any reason whatsoever. Prince [Alphonse Gabriel Octave] Broglio was also chastised. We postponed our retribution until the evening when a thunderstorm was supposed to unfold above his [Kriedener's] head. Upon arriving at the bivouac, all the officers of the regiment met their battalion commanders and told them that they intend to ask the regimental commander Colonel Kriedener to bring to the attention of the Grand Duke, that the officers, no longer willing to endure ill-treatment from their commander, appeal to have him restrained. Consequently, battalion commanders Colonel Posnikov, Pisarev, and Baron de Damas went to Kriedener, and Colonel Posnikov announced that, as required by [Kriedener's] order, after a 24 hour deliberation, he and his comrades-in-arms were there to inform him that his officers did not change their minds, but, on the contrary, together with all officers of the two remaining battalions, they now insist that this affair be reported to the Grand Duke himself. Colonel Pisarev's companions, in turn, repeated the same thing. Colonel Kriedener, enraged, was forced to go immediately with a report to the Grand Duke. (The emperor had long endorsed the officers' courts, and through them many scoundrels were removed from the regiment. Kriedener fully deserved the same fate.) The joy was universal, despite the fact that this affair could take a bad turn. Prince Golitsyn was the ring leader.

10 [22] July. Wednesday.

Camp at Pogorelets. Our corps was on the road from 5 am until 3 pm. It was raining throughout this time. This march, although relatively short, was nevertheless quite arduous. As soon as we reached the bivouac, the grand duke arrived on horseback, soaking wet and covered with mud, and ordered to gather all officers. Restless, he did not wait until all officers gathered and, by the time I arrived, he had already begun to talk. Here are the details of this event: the great duke dismounted from his horse, which was then held by his side. He was surrounded by officers and spoke calmly and evenly. Colonel Kriedener stood on the side, just as the horse of the Grand Duke did. He had the appearance of a visitor from the nether world. "Gentlemen, - said the Grand Duke as I approached, - the enemy is in the center of our state. He had occupied six provinces in a single offensive. Is it possible, at this time of danger, to bring up matters of personal ambition? Remember that you must set an example for the army. Remember that you are Russian nobles, and you should have only one thought, one desire - to save your homeland from the danger, which, I will not conceal it from you, is threatening her. The first duty of a military man - to obey, even if he has a stone for a commander (at these words he looked at Kriedener, who was probably not particularly flattered at such a comparison). You, battalion commanders, are spoiling your young officers a bit too much, especially you, Baron de Damas (among the battalion commanders, Kriedener liked Baron de Damas the least, the two had a confrontation at the camp at Svencionys, and the Grand Duke, remembering it now, repeated the whole criticism of Baron de Damas in subtle terms). You, M. Khrapovitskii, if you felt insulted by the colonel, should not have let the whole cadre of officers to come to your defense, and should have demanded satisfaction yourself. However, I believe that the colonel was right and you deserve a severe reprimand; (then the grand duke then turned addressing everyone,), I beg you and hope, gentlemen, that you will stop this disorder, and, remembering that any rallies are prohibited by law, will realize your misconduct of revolting against your own commander, and will seek to make amends for this transgression through exemplary service. I repeat, one must obey even a stone if placed under its command. Perchance, I feel this myself as I speak to you since I have to submit to someone who should be under my command (a hint to a discord between the grand duke and army commander-in-chief Barclay de Tolly). I beseech you, gentlemen, to obey your commander and do not forget that now is the wartime and misconduct is punishable by death. M.

Khrapovitskii deserves death [for his misconduct] and the sole reason he is not executed yet is [my] lenience. Good-bye, gentlemen, and, for my sake, put an end to this mess, which is very distressing to the sovereign."

"For you, Your Highness, we will do everything," cried all officers at once. The Grand Duke had mounted his horse already and, as he rode away, he shouted to us from afar: "And for the colonel, gentlemen." Following this, Colonel Kriedener came up to us, and addressed Colonel Posnikov, the most senior officer after him, with the following words: "Colonel, I do not want to command a unit that acts in such a manner towards me so I relegate my authority to you." All officers led by Colonel Pisarev, the most senior colonel after Posnikov, appealed to the latter with an expression of joy to be under his command. Colonel Kriedener, who made just a few steps away, quickly returned and told Colonel Posnikov that he was reclaiming his authority in order to give himself the pleasure of punishing chief instigators of all these machinations against him. "Colonel Pisarev, - he said - Give me your sword, I arrest you." Officers, who have already begun to disperse, immediately returned, and Prince Golitsyn inquired, "Why are you, colonel, arresting Colonel Pisarev, we all here are as guilty as he is..." However, Colonel Kriedener interrupted him and asked for his sword as well. Baron [Captain Peter] Frederix wanted to say a few words, but suffered the same fate. Then several people began to talk at once. Unable to continue arresting people, Kriedener mounted his horse and galloped after the Grand Duke. Before returning to our tents, we decided not to abandon our friends and share their fate. The rest of the day was spent in an agony of oblivion, while Pisarev, Golitsyn and Frederix went to the *hauptwache*.

11 [23] July. Thursday.

Camp near Vitebsk. Our corps again departed at 5 o'clock in the morning, crossed the Dvina River near Vitebsk and camped out with the rest of the 1st Western Army immediately outside the city. The commander appeared at the head of the regiment but he had such a gloomy appearance which had never been seen before on him. He did not utter a word during the entire march. Apparently, he got his due.

12 [24] July. Friday.

Standing still. The Grand Duke ordered to return swords to Pisarev, Golitsyn and Frederix. Kriedener removed Pisarev from commanding our battalion but then claimed illness and left, relegating his authority to Colonel Posnikov. A little later, General Baron Rosen restored Pisarev as a battalion commander, to our joy. The Grand Duke was soon ordered to leave the army and return to the [Imperial] court, and our corps was entrusted to Lieutenant-General [Nikolai] Lavrov. The 4th Corps departed tonight.

13 [25] July. Saturday.

Standing still. At 9:00 we heard the sound of cannon fire from the direction of Ostrovno, where the 4th Corps was engaged on battle. By 11 o'clock, the sound of gunfire approached us and we, officers, were ordered to return from the city, where we went for lunch, told not to leave anywhere and be ready to fight. All of our corps' cavalry was sent to support Count [Alexander] Osterman [-Tolstoy], who commanded the 4th Corps. By evening we were expecting an order to depart but did not receive it.

14 [26] July. Sunday.

The enemy is approaching Vitebsk. Fighting resumed in the morning. We moved to our left flank and stopped in the reserve almost directly in front of the city. The fighting was desperate. The 4th Corps fought in the front line throughout this time [and] we were not committed to any combat. The fighting stopped as the night descended and we fell asleep under full arms. Kriedener, believing that the regiment would be sent to battle, appeared before the regiment to share our fate on the battlefield. He was a very pitiful sight to behold.

15 [27] July. Monday.

Camp at Korolevo, some 20 *versta*s from Vitebsk. I woke up very late. The enemy retreated for some eight *versta*s. Our rearguard had a few fights at dawn. Our corps departed before noon, leaving its bivouac at Vitebsk, in which bridges and barns were already in flames. While our rearguard retreated, our corps went to Korolevo on the way from Vitebsk to Smolensk, where it stopped. We continued this withdrawal to connect with the 2nd Western Army for joint operations.

16 [28] July. Tuesday.

Camp at Lyozno. We marched from 5 am to 2 pm. No firing was heard. At 9 pm, an alarm signal was sounded instead of the one for dawn. We immediately prepared, but after receiving no further orders, went to sleep in full combat ammunition. Suck tricks, apparently, were to Lavrov's liking.

17-19 [29-31] July. From Wednesday to Friday.

Camp near Smolensk. We left Lyozno during the night from Tuesday to Wednesday, after 1 am. Passing Rudnya, we moved for another 4 *versta*s before halting for several hours. We were allowed to cook soup. We were told that we will have only brief stops and not night rests until we reach Smolensk. Before 10 pm, we were again broke our camp and then stopped to rest after midnight. After a 2 hour respite during the night from Wednesday to Thursday, we were back on the road and entered the province of Smolensk. This is the center of Russia, and we have [now] transplanted our troops here. We made a brief halt on Thursday morning to cook some soup, and, at 5 pm, we moved again, continuing our march without interruption until nightfall. We then made another halt around 1 am during the night from Thursday to Friday and then continued our journey. In the morning we were allowed yet another respite, and shortly after noon we finally encamped some four *versta*s from Smolensk. One can only imagine how exhausted by hunger and fatigue we had been after such forced marches. I was very glad to receive permission to go to Smolensk, where I stayed until dawn. The only remaining tavern had a brisk business that day. The Grand Duke returned to resume command of our corps. In Smolensk, I met [Colonel of LG Preobrazhenskii Regiment Nikanor] Svechin with his wife, who were making their way from Grodno to Moscow. Just one month ago they met Madame B. and brought me great pleasure by talking about her.

20 July [1 August]. Saturday.

The next morning I suddenly realized that I had lost a wallet with 200 rubles. This amount, though not particularly significant, required me to be extra guarded, and the loss saddened me very much.

21 July [2 August]. Sunday.

I received beautiful watches from Madame B. Her silence, however, continues.

22 and 23 July [3-4 August]. Monday and Tuesday.

Standing still. A thanksgiving service to mark the Sovereign's saint's day was held in the camps. I again spent entire day in Smolensk. The 2nd Western Army of Prince Bagration joined ours. We can expect now some decisive actions. We are all eager to fight, each of us is ready to shed our blood to the very last drop, and if we are commanded well, we will inflict great harm to the enemy. The new military law is very severe, today two men were shot for looting. We had to send one man from each company to be present at the executions.

24 July [5 August]. Wednesday.

Everyone is still in place. The Grand Duke assumed his command and visited our camp accompanied by Prince Bagration. We deployed by battalions to greet our leaders.

25 July [6 August]. Thursday.

Still in places. We learned about the victory achieved by Count Wittgenstein's corps over Marshal Oudinot at Polotsk; the enemy lost 5,000 killed and 2,000 captured.

26 July [7 August]. Friday.

Camp at Prykaz-Vydra. Because of the enemy's retreat, we marched at 5 am and headed for the road that went to Vitebsk. After 20 *versta*s, we halted in battalion columns.

27 July [8 August]. Saturday.

Camp on the road to Porechye. We were supposed to leave our positions at 5 am, but due to new orders we remained in place until 8 pm. Having deployed in columns, we again returned to the Smolensk road, and after passing 5-6 *versta*s in this direction, we halted to rest. Three hours later we marched again, passing two *versta*s before turning off road to the left. The darkness was terrible. My horse (we were recently allowed to have two horses) stumbled continually. The rain and lack of sleep exhausted us. And so we went throughout the night from Saturday to Sunday. We walked along a dirt road through the forest. The darkness and the rain intensified, and our situation became intolerable. Having reached the road which runs from Smolensk to Porechye, we again made a halt until dawn. Then we moved another 10 *versta*s towards Porechye and bivouacked by battalions. Platov, who remained in his previous position, had a battle with the enemy [at Molevo Boloto], and took 1,000 prisoners.

28 July [9 August]. Sunday.

Standing still.

29 July [10 August]. Monday.

Standing still. Most of our army has caught up with us.

30 July [11 August]. Tuesday.

Standing still. The first order, to depart at 8 pm, was canceled. We again developed a fondness for tents, so I also bought a very small one, which can always be set up very quickly, whereas building a hovel always requires more time.

31 July [12 August]. Wednesday.

Standing still. The other day (July 27) General Sebastiani's own carriage was captured. People say that notes were found in his portfolio of notes, which included numbers and places as well as daily movements of our corps. Rumors have it that, because of this, all suspicious persons were removed from the main headquarters, among them flügel-adjutant and counts: [Colonel Wladislaw] Branicki, [Colonel Slanislaus] Potocki, [Colonel Mikhail] Vlodeck and the commander-in-chief's own adjutant [Baron Vladimir] Löwenstern (the Swede).

AUGUST

1 [13] August. Thursday.

Our inexperience in military affairs clearly manifests itself at every step. The order to move to Shelomets, the village that we passed on the night of 27 to 28, was given to the 3rd and 6th Corps at the same time, as well as to the 2nd and 3rd Cavalry Divisions, while our 5th Corps was to make after all of these units. Instead of ensuring that people are not exhausted, they do just the opposite. Our corps, placed under arms at 4 pm, immediately left the Porechye road but after an hour long march had to stop to pass other units that should have been ahead of us. Consequently, we were moved too early which deprived the soldiers a few hours of rest, which they so badly needed. It would have been much better not to move us from our positions at all since, after moving for five *versta*s, we had to stop for the night. I could not relax because I was on duty.

2 [14] August. Friday.

Camp about 30 *versta*s from Smolensk, on the road to Rudnya. Our 5th Corps was able to depart only at 4 am, passed through Shelomets, reached its previous bivouacs at Prikaz-Vydra and then moved further along the Smolensk road. Mud and disadvantage of moving in the wake of a large column greatly delayed our march. We reached our bivouac only late at night and in complete darkness. During the day, a certain woman came to our column and told everyone who asked who she was that she belonged to General Lavrov. Everyone was satisfied with such an answer until one lad tried to make advances to her and, in a fit of passion, tore her hat, finding a male head under it. It turned out that he was a spy sent to the main headquarters.

3 [15] August. Saturday.

Standing still. Yesterday's incident with a spy forced me to be vigilant. Noticing today a certain person, dressed in city clothing, who was walking in our camp and asking around where the Grand Duke was sting, I arrested him at once and sent him to the duty officer. We can hear sound of gunfire from the direction of Smolensk.

4 [16] August. Sunday.

Instead of morning dawn, an alarm was sounded today. It was the signal to depart - and off we went at 9 o'clock in the morning. Our corps went to Smolensk, and about five *versta*s from the city, it turned to the left and pitched camp, by battalions, on the road to Porechye, with the city directly in front of us. The battle for Smolensk lasted the entire day, with the enemy advancing along the road from Krasnyi. We reached our positions only by 10 pm and under the moonlight. Madame B. sent me a very nice small flashlight, which I used for the first time today.

5 [17] August. Monday.

The battle was resumed at dawn, the fighting took place next to the city walls. Both sides fought fiercely. All units gradually departed, and in the evening, only our corps remained in the reserve, standing in its position on the road to Porechye. Interested in the course of the battle, I went to Smolensk, to the place where the fiercest battle was fought. Admiring the courage and bravery of our troops, I still came to a sad conclusion that we would soon yield the city. I saw the brave general Dokhturov in the most dangerous place under heavy cross-fire at the gates of Smolensk. The streets of the suburbs were crowded with corpses, fur hats of French grenadiers and different weapons. This was clear evidence that the enemy several times burst into the suburbs, and each time he was driven back by our troops. Soon fire broke out in several parts of the city and lasted longer than the battle itself, which ended by the nightfall and was replaced by artillery duel which continued unabated throughout the night. Smolensk was still ours. The Guard jagers occupied a suburb on the right bank of the Dnieper.

6 [18] August. Tuesday.

When we awoke, the whole city was in flames. At 9 am, we received orders to retreat. Our corps, after moving for nine *versta*s along the road to Porechye, stopped and rested until 7 pm. Marching once again, the corps moved for a few more *versta*s down the road to Porechye and, after passing the place where we spent the night on the 29th, it stopped overnight at Prudische. Everyone dined poorly because of lack of bread.

7 [19] August. Wednesday.

At dawn, the 5th and 6th corps proceeded on the road to Dorogobuzh and stopped 70 *versta*s [46 miles] from this city. The soldiers were allowed to undress and cavalrymen to unsaddle horses.

8 [20] August. Thursday.

Continuing to retreat, our corps departed at 1 am during the night from the 7th to the 8th. We moved for 45 *versta*s [30 miles], crossed on pontoon bridge to the left bank of the Dnieper at Pnievy and stopped at

Ustrom. The entire First Army was moving in this direction. We were very glad to bivouac next to the river and bathed as much as we could.

9 [21] August. Friday.

Camp at Usvyatye. Departing at 9 o'clock in the morning, we stopped in a vast valley at Usvyatye. This was once a battlefield, where many people died in the battle between the Russian and Poles. Count [Heraclius] de Polignac asked a French officer prisoner, how long ago he had left France. "Only three days ago," he responded. Seeing the count's bewilderment, the Frenchman observed, "Of course, three days, does not Smolensk belong to France now?"

10 [22] August. Saturday.

Everything pointed to a major battle at Usvyatye. An order to prepare for battle was already issued but, at 3 pm, just as we moved to take up positions, we were ordered to depart at dusk. About five *versta*s from Dorogobuzh, we were stopped and not allowed to undress, instead told to wait for new orders, which we never received. Here our pack horses caught up with us. I was very glad to see my driver looking for my horse.

11 [23] August. Sunday.

Waking up, I was surprised that we are on the same site, though the sun was already high in the sky. The Second Army, positioned behind ours, was moving to get ahead of us, so we could not move until it has passed, which lasted until 8 am. We took up positions that we had abandoned at 3 pm the previous day; it is obvious that it would have been better to just let us have a good night sleep. By 7 o'clock in the evening we could hear gunfire in the advance guard so we had to change positions and move on to the road a few *versta*s from our former position. Our new position was very disadvantageous - our front to the Second Army, and the rear facing the enemy. A decisive battle is expected.

From 12 [24] to 15 [27] August. From Monday to Thursday.

On Monday I was a duty officer and constantly conveyed orders to the regiment to be ready to change positions. This uncertainty lasted until 8 o'clock in the evening when we finally moved, but not to redeploy to a new position, but to make a 12-hour march on the road from Dorogobuzh to Vyazma. On Monday evening, as we passed through

Dorogobuzh, we were struck by its gloomy atmosphere. The city was completely empty. We only found one woman with 3 children, who fled from a village that was first occupied by the French and then devastated and plundered by Cossacks. The poor woman was in tears. We gave her some money, for which she was very grateful. After marching all night long from Monday to Tuesday, we stopped some thirty *versta*s away from Dorogobuzh, stood there until 6 pm and then continued our march in the same direction. At 2 o'clock in the night from Tuesday to Wednesday, we encamped some 25 *versta*s [16.5 miles] from Vyazma. Here we received the commander-in-chief's order not to march during the day, but for some strange twist of fate we were always forced to do the opposite. His Excellency would order us to stand still - we moved; we were ordered to move - we stood; finally, if we were told that we would soon enter a battle, we, in all probability, did not fight. As a consequence, we no longer believed the orders received from Barclay de Tolly, and we did not believe his order this time either. In fact, we departed at 8 pm on the 14th and marched all night long. A halt for rest at 1 am. Luka told me the sad news that one of my horses (I had two) escaped. This was my favorite horse, which, in addition, kissed Madame B. on the day of my departure from Pulkovo. This horse was very precious for me, so I cursed at Luka and spent the rest of the day in a bad mood. On the 15th, in the morning, we were at Vyazma, passed the town and after moving for another two *versta*s, encamped on the Moscow road. Because the commander-in-chief made no promises to us, we remained relaxed for the entire day.

16 [28] August. Friday.

We finally managed to spend the entire night in one place. At 1 pm we received orders to move in the direction of Moscow. We stopped some 10 *versta*s [6.6 miles] from Vyazma and 29 *versta*s [20 miles] from Teplukhi. You could hear the sound of gunfire coming from Vyazma and see the fire burning inside the town. The Grand Duke again left us.

17 [29] August. Saturday.

Camp near Tsarevo Zaimysche. Drums awoke us at 3:30 am, when we least expected it. We immediately set off and soon were some nine *versta*s beyond Teplukhi. There, short distance from Tsarevo Zaimysche, where the main army headquarters was located, we were deployed, by battalions, in battle formation. Prince [Mikhail] Kutuzov, who was appointed commander of all armies, arrived here today.

18 [30] August. Sunday.

Camp at Gzhatsk. Before leaving Tsarevo Zaimysche we hoped to see Prince Kutuzov in our camp, but he did not come and we were ordered to depart at 12 o'clock. By 8:30 pm we were already some four *versta*s beyond Gzhatsk and pitched a camp. Gzhatsk - a beautiful little town. Its buildings are mostly of wood, constructed with great taste. It is painful and hurtful to know that these graceful buildings will become prey to the fire in the very near future.

19 [31] August. Monday.

Standing still. The sound of gunfire can be heard in the rearguard. Prince Kutuzov visited our camp and this visit greatly pleased us. Called up to command the army by the will of the people and almost against the wishes of the emperor, he enjoys universal confidence in the army.

20 August [1 September]. Tuesday.

Camp on the 21st *versta* [14 miles] from Gzhatsk. The annoying drum woke us up at 3:30 am. The corps marched at once in the same direction on the road to Moscow. We stopped at 8:30 am on the 41st *versta* [27 miles] from Gzhatsk.

21 August [2 September]. Wednesday.

At the camp at the Kolotsk Monastery.

22 August [3 September]. Thursday.

Our corps departed at 6 am, entered the Moscow province and pitched camp at Borodino at 10 o'clock in the morning. We expect an enemy attack on these positions. You could hear a strong gunfire in the vanguard. We learned yesterday that a French detachment of 200 men attacked the peasants of Prince Golitsyn in the woods where they have been hiding. The peasants repulsed this attack, killing some 45 enemy men and capturing another 50. It is remarkable that even women fought fiercely on this occasion. Among the dead is an eighteen-year old girl who fought especially valiantly and, upon receiving a mortal wounded, she still had the will power to stab a Frenchman who shot her, and died having avenged herself.

23 August [4 September]. Friday.

Standing still.

24 August [5 September]. Saturday.

Our left wing under the command of Prince Bagration was involved in the battle [at Shevardino], which lasted until the nightfall. As the battle unfolded, a mass for the God's blessing of our troops and granting us victory in the upcoming battle was held in the camp. As a duty officer, I was ordered to allow soldiers to remove their knapsacks and unfurl their overcoats.

25 August [6 September]. Sunday.

At 11 am we changed positions. The jagers occupied forward outposts, the rest of the corps moved slightly to the left and forward for about a *versta* and a half. We were directly in front of enemy and in complete inaction. I personally went forward to the great battery to inspect the enemy's positions. The terrain was fairly open, and, standing on the elevation, one could see most of both armies. They stood face to face, as if frozen. [Artillery commander] General [Karl] Löwenstern, whom I found on the battery, ordered to fire a gun. The cannonball tore through the air, flew between enemy sentries, but there was no response to this challenge.

26 August [7 September]. Monday.

The Battle of Borodino. At 5:30 am our corps was already under arms and moved slightly forward. We deployed in battle formation by battalions. At dawn we heard gunshots. Our position was in the bushes. The Guard jagers soon joined us. The cavalry and our 2nd Brigade (the Izmailovskii and Lithuanian regiments) were detached and moved to the left. The cavalry made several brilliant attacks, and our infantry, formed a square, repelled several charges of the enemy cavalry. However, our jagers, who joined us in the morning, deserved a reprimand for their carelessness and inattention at the outposts which allowed the enemy to cause great harm to them; they lost a lot of people without inflicting almost any damage onto the French. Our brigade, consisting of the Semeyonovskii and Preobrazhenskii regiments, remained under enemy's heavy artillery bombardment for fourteen hours straight. It has stood steadfastly with imperturbable coolness, which the elite units should possess. By the evening the enemy had made such a success that the bullets of skirmishers began to reach us; nevertheless, we maintained our position and remained in the position we occupied for the night. My company lost thirty five men.

27 August [8 September]. Tuesday.

We remained on the battle field until two o'clock during the night from Monday to Tuesday. Then our brigade moved to Mozhaisk, where it joined the rest of the corps and bivouacked behind the town. Upon seeing the Lithuanians [Life Guard Lithuanian Regiment], I hastened to inquire about the fate of my brother Nicholas. Some said that [a cannonball] tore off his foot, others that he was only wounded by a bullet. [Fortunately] the latter report was confirmed. The former information, however, was somewhat correct as well since a distant relative of mine, also Nicholas, lost a leg.[25] By 6 o'clock in the evening we once again heard gunfire in the rearguard.

28 August [9 September]. Wednesday.

During the night from Tuesday to Wednesday we departed at 2 am and, after covering some 19 *versta*s [12.5 miles] from Mozhaisk along the Moscow road, we stopped for a bivouac. The cannonade, which we initially heard from afar, gradually approached us by the evening but we still remained in place. General Platov, who commanded the rearguard, reported that the enemy was still far off, but then unexpectedly brought him to our positions, causing Prince Kutuzov to hastily retreat with the main headquarters.

29 August [10 September]. Thursday.

We marched from 2 am to 9 am and stopped some 63 *versta*s [41.5 miles] from Moscow. General Platov was removed from commanding the rearguard.

30 August [11 September]. Friday.

Bivouac at Vyazemy. Yesterday, the rearguard had a major action against the enemy [near the village of Krymskoe]. We were ready to depart

---

[25] Pushin refers to Lieutenant Nikolai Nikolaevich Pushin of the Life Guard Lithuanian Regiment, who lost his leg to a cannonball and was awarded the Order of St. Anna (2nd class). Pushin's cousin was wounded by a bullet in the left leg and was awarded a golden sword for courage.

at any moment but moved only at 1 am on Thursday. We walked until 11 o'clock in the morning on the 30th and stopped some 35 *versta*s from Moscow, at a very beautiful house in Vyazemy. I fell asleep at 6 pm. These nocturnal marches greatly exhaust us.

31 August [12 September]. Saturday.

We marched at 4 o'clock in the morning, stopped about 6 *versta*s from Moscow. The view of our ancient capital had a profound impression on us and everyone desired to win or die under its walls. Each of us was burning with a desire to save our holy city, our Russian hero.

SEPTEMBER

1 [13] September. Sunday.

At 4 o'clock in the morning we changed our positions, redeploying to about two *versta*s from the city of Moscow, resting with our right flank on the main road. After receiving permission to go to Moscow, which I have never seen before, I went to dine there. The town was almost empty. Only a few commoners remain in it. My uncle [Actual State Counselor Stepan Pushin] has left as well, so I could not get any information about the status of my brother Nicholas. After a miserable lunch at the London tavern on the Tverskaya Street, one of the main streets of Moscow, I returned back to the camp through the Dorogomilov gates.

2 [14] September. Monday.

To our surprise, at 4 o'clock in the morning, we moved to Moscow, entered it through the Dorogomilov gates and then departed form it through the Vladimir gates. The population, almost entirely drunk, ran after us reproaching us for leaving the capital without a fight. Many have joined our columns in order to leave the town before the enemy arrived. This sight wrung our hearts. On leaving the city we moved to the Ryazan road and walked for 17 *versta*s before halting. During the march, I saw my brother Nicholas. The wound was not dangerous, he was on his way to Kasimov. He was shot through the thigh by a bullet, so he needed to consult a surgeon for treatment. I also met [retired Major General Alexei]

Avdulin, who left St. Petersburg on August 26. Prior to his departure he met my sisters and Madame B. and I was delighted to talk to him about our mutual friends.

3 [15] September. Tuesday.

Standing still. The news of the French occupation of Moscow aroused a widespread indignation, and caused such grumbling among us that many officers declared that if peace is concluded [with Napoleon], they would leave to serve in Spain.

4 [16] September. Wednesday.

Camp at Kulakovo, near the Myachikov mound. We departed at 3 am, everyone in the direction of Ryazan. We bivouacked near the Myachikov mound on the Moscow River. In the evening we heard a strong but brief cannonade.

5 [17] September. Thursday and Friday the 6th [18 September].

Camp at Podolsk. On Thursday, at 4 o'clock, we were forced to march again and, after moving ten *versta*s from Kulakovo, we were ordered to turn right off the main road to Ryazan and proceeded by force marches in the new direction. We walked all night from the 5th to the 6th and stopped only at 9 am on Friday in Podolsk, a small town located on the Moscow-Tula road. During this march, I ran away. Sleep overcame me to such an extent that I could not endure it anymore. At 1 am I traveled ahead [of my troops] and upon reaching the first village, I fell fast asleep there. Waking up only at 6 o'clock in the morning, I was pleasantly surprised that our corps stopped near the village where I found a shelter for the night.

7 [19] September. Saturday.

Standing still. (After passing Podolsk).

8 [20] September. Sunday.

Camp at the village of Krasnaya Pakhra. We marched since 4:30 am until 1 o'clock in the afternoon. Continuing our maneuver to the left flank, we left the main road to Tula and moved on local paths to the Kaluga road which we reached at Krasnaya Pakhra. [I stopped at] a delightful country gentlemen's house. An unexpected good fortune fell to my lot today. Only someone who is familiar with a campaign life can truly appreciate the happiness I felt today. As our corps was deployed for a bivouac, my company found itself stationed next to the village. Taking full advantage of this, I quickly obtained an apartment. It is true that the house has no doors or windows, but still this was a room by itself; generals occupied the best rooms and I naturally could not claim them.

9 [21] September. Monday.

Standing still. I was fortunate to find another, much warmer, room. All officers from our battalion spent the entire day with me, which greatly pleased me.

10 [22] September. Tuesday.

To change position, we moved back for two *versta*s to the Kaluga road. The main headquarters stayed at Krasnaya Pakhra. This movement had no strategic value whatsoever, yet it seemed to be purposefully undertaken to cause me problems by depriving me of my apartment.

11 [23] September. Wednesday.

Standing still. A cannonade which we heard today alerted us to the start of a battle in which our rear guard was involved. We were ordered to be prepared for battle.

12 [24] September. Thursday.

Standing still.

13 [25] September. Friday.

Standing still. We can see fires in the distance. This is Moscow burning. In the evening we observed a celestial phenomenon. As I was resting in my tent, Luka called to show me something. It was a fiery and pointed band that quickly rose over the glow of the fire, and soon disappeared without a trace. Obviously, it was the result of the fire, but this did not prevent people from interpreting it as a portent of something, but they could not decide whether that something was good or bad.

14 [26] September. Saturday.

Again, at 8 am, we changed positions, moving one *versta* to the right.

15 [27] September. Sunday.

Camp at Babinki, near Voronov. At 3:30 am our corps marched, continuing its retreat along the Kaluga road. It stopped at Babinki, not far from Voronov. I was chilled and under the pretext of seeing General Dokhturov, who was in the village with his staff, I went to him to warm up.

16 [28] September. Monday.

We were again ordered to be ready for battle. Our cavalry rushed forward, but soon returned, and we remained in place. After dinner I again went to Dokhturov, and spent the night [at the village.]

17 [29] September. Tuesday.

To escape idleness, to which we were doomed in the camp, I went to Dokhturov to play cards, but paid dearly for this – I lost all my money.

18 [30] September. Wednesday.

Another order to prepare for battle, and once again nothing happened. We remain in place. I was again on duty in the division. This is, as a rule, a colonel's duty, but because colonels are lacking, captains served in their stead. [Captain of Life Guard Izmailovskii Regiment Nikolai] Somov came to dine with me, and I received letters from St. Petersburg, which greatly pleased me.

19 September [1 October]. Thursday.

Camp at Spasskoe. We departed at 3 am and stopped at 10 o'clock, after marching for 13 *versta*s in the direction of Kaluga. As soon we reached Spasskoe, I encountered a certain Mr. Levin. He left St. Petersburg on 8 August and brought me letters from my sisters which delighted me.

20 September [2 October]. Friday.

Standing still. The rearguard had a major fight [today].

21 September [3 October]. Saturday.

The troops departed at 5 o'clock in the morning. The weather was wonderful - we have not had such a lovely weather in a long time. Our corps, continuing to retreat, marched for 12 *versta*s on the same Kaluga road, crossed the Nara River and stopped between Tarutino and Letashevka. The main headquarters of Prince Kutuzov also moved there.

22 September [4 October]. Sunday.

The rearguard was engaged in a combat today, we are expecting a general battle so we will wait here for an enemy who, apparently, wants to move forward.

23 September [5 October]. Monday.

A mass was held for blessings for the upcoming battle, for which we were preparing. In the evening we received orders to extinguish all lights in the camp because French general, Adjutant General [Jacques Alexander] Lauriston, was supposed to arrive for a meeting with Prince Kutuzov.

24 September [6 October]. Tuesday.

We know nothing so far the yesterday's meeting [between Kutuzov and Lauriston]. Prince [Peter] Volkonskii, who arrived directly from the Emperor to the headquarters, was present at the meeting. Some claim that peace would be soon concluded.

26 September [8 October]. Thursday.

Rumor spread that the French are threatening to attack us but, as it is accepted, suspend hostilities while truce talks are conducted. We took several prisoners.

27 September [9 October]. Friday.

Letters from St. Petersburg ariived today and I am very happy. My family already knows about the battle [of Borodino] on August 26th and that I was not wounded.

28 September [10 October]. Saturday.

We are still sitting quietly in one place, but we cannot say the same about our partisans. They are constantly making incursions, causing much damage to the enemy and taking many prisoners. The *feldfebel* of my company, who was promoted to an officer just a few days ago, dined with me today. You cannot imagine how embarrassed he was by this honor. I was very amused.[26]

29 September [11 October]. Sunday.

So far our parades proceeded without any [formal] ceremonies, but today's order changed that, it seems pedantry is prevailing.

30 September [12 October]. Monday.

We dug burrows in the ground well so our soldiers can set up bath houses.

OCTOBER

1 [13] October. Tuesday.

The cold made itself felt, so I decided to build a barrack, which was completed in 3 hours. Its base was lowered for entire *arshin* [over two feet] into the ground, and the kettle pot provided excellent heating. I was as happy as one could be in our position. Order was issued prohibiting anyone from leaving the camp because of the expected departure, consequently, I had to bid farewell to my beautiful housing.

2 [14] October. Wednesday.

Yesterday's order was repeated again today. However after a few hours later soldiers were allowed to bathe. My company's turn finally arrived and, since I had two officers, I suggested Chicherin to lead the company. He declined claiming he was ill so I was forced to escort my men in

---

[26] Author later added the following note: "In 1848 Feldfebel Ivan Alekseev, with the rank of staff officer, served as a warden of exercise-house in the Engineers' Castle."

person. Chicherin and I had an argument [over this]. Our baths were in Tarutino. I was amazed to see that, in fifteen days, the village was completely destroyed. Upon returning to the camp I was told that I was awarded the Order of St. Vladimir for the battle of Borodino. Somov came from the headquarters specifically to tell me about it.

4 [16] October. Thursday.

I dined with Somov at Letashevka and as soon as I returned to the barracks, I was ordered to get dressed. It seemed the departure as inevitable, but it did not happen. Instead, we received a different order – to get ready for an inspection tomorrow.

5 [17] October. Saturday.

Since early morning we stood under arms for inspection. The general has not yet managed to get to our battalion when it began to rain heavily, a good thing to dispel our indolence. We were ordered to return to barracks. After lunch, having received official notice of my award, I borrowed the Order of St. Vladimir from a senior officer, put it on and was very pleased. We soon received a new order from which we learned that we were supposed to attack the enemy, or rather, we were supposed to make unexpected attack on the French avant-garde, under the command of the King of Naples [Joachim Murat], which occupied position on the other side of the Nara River, near Tarutino. As a consequence, our corps marched at 10 pm, and stopped after passing Tarutino, still undetected by enemy outposts. At these positions, we rested. We are allowed to lie down, but to make no noise or light any fires till dawn.

6 [18] October. Sunday.

Attack. Our offensive began at 6 am, when the enemy least expected it. General Count [Vasily] Orlov-Denisov and his Cossacks completely overwhelmed it. General [Levin] Benningsen attacked the left flank, and we attacked in the center. We met almost no resistance and pressed the attack without stopping. The French could not resist such pressure and rushed into the forest by 12 pm. Our light troops pursued them while our corps stopped to rest. At the very beginning of the battle we lost General [Karl] Baggovut, a cannonball cut him in half. Yet we captured plenty of French prisoners and 33 guns. It is believed that the [French] had lost two generals, of whom one is captured and another killed. During a halt I went to inspect the French camp. There were numerous dead horse lying around, their thighs cut out, probably for food. Everything indicated that these gentlemen did not enjoy the same excess of provisions as we do at Tarutino. At 5 o'clock in the evening, our corps returned to its barracks. The joy was universal. The soldiers sang songs throughout the march. I was thrilled to see our barracks and fell asleep with a light heart.

7 [19] October. Monday.

We held a thanksgiving service on the occasion of yesterday's victory. Another 500 prisoners were captured, including [Neapolitan] General Dery [Murat's aide-de-camp]. I started to rebuild my quarters, and because I wanted to allow myself some luxury, I had to had to be patient and sleep one night under the open sky.

8 [20] October. Tuesday.

It is alleged that a French negotiator met with Prince Kutuzov. My barrack has been completed, and it turned out quite good, you can actually spend the winter inside it.

9 [21] October. Wednesday.

Review, which was interrupted by the rain on the 5th, was held today. It is already getting quite cold.

10 [22] October. Thursday.

When you have basic necessities, you desire to treat yourself to some luxury. Today, my shelter was given a fashionable appearance. It was decorated with pine branches, and two tree trunks, serving as columns, were set up at the entrance. It turned out very nicely. Hardly had I admired the results of this enterprise as all of units began to depart and people say our corps will be next. This means all my exertion was in vain.

11 [23] October. Friday.

Finally, at 3 pm today, we left our camp at Tarutino, where we spent 20 days, during which abundance of food and good barracks revived the troops, frequent reviews straightened them while the corps were brought up to strength. Our corps marched through Letashevka and Ugodskii Zavod and moved late into the night until the darkness forced us to stop.

I had to sleep under the open sky because we were not allowed to set up barracks.

12 [24] October. Saturday.

The 5th Corps departed at 8 am in the direction of Maloyaroslavets, where the 6th Corps has already engaged the enemy. We reached the battlefield at 3 pm, and crossed the battlefield under cover of our batteries and took up positions in the back of the line. The city was in flames, our jagers fought vigorously. The battle lasted all day long. At nightfall, the men were allowed to lie down to rest, but the batteries did not cease firing.

13 [25] October. Sunday.

We woke up when the firing stopped. At 5 am our corps marched hastily for four *versta*s from Maloyaroslavets toward Medyn. We can hear gunfire on the left [wing]. It is probably the enemy moving his forces to Borovsk. No one stayed in the ruins of Maloyaroslavets. Some eleven guns, captured by Platov, were brought into our camp.

14 [26] October. Monday.

Camp in Goncharovo. After departing at 4:30 in the morning, we proceeded on the road to Kaluga and encamped on the eighteenth *versta*s from Maloyaroslavets, near the village of Goncharovo. Our position is thirty seven *versta*s away from Kaluga. We could hear gunfire all night long – it is General Platov pursuing the enemy and moving to the Medyn.

15 [27] October. Tuesday.

We held a mass on the occasion of presentation of the icon of Our Lady by the Kursk nobility. At 3:00 pm our corps again marched on the Kaluga road, and, in a few *versta*s, turned off to the right, moving on country roads until late at night when darkness forced us to stop. It was very cold; I lay so close to the fire that almost completely burned my coat.

16 [28] October. Wednesday.

Our halt proved to be brief. At 2 am we moved forward once again. At 7 am we reached the linen manufactory located on the road from

Kaluga to Medyn where we stopped. The enemy is retreating everywhere and is daily losing [more and more] guns.

17 [29] October. Thursday.

At 12 pm we departed in the direction of Medyn, then bivouacked near the village of Adamovskaya. Along the way we came across two guns abandoned by the French.

18 [30] October. Friday.

After leaving at 4 am, we kept moving forward. From Medyn we headed to Mozhaisk and stopped about three *versta*s from the village of Kremenskaya. Passing through Medyn, we stopped to rest. There were many dead bodies, among which I saw the corpse of a young woman.

19 [31] October. Saturday.

We were on the road since 4 am until late at night. We moved by country road leading to Vyazma, stopped for bivouac at the Spasskoye. Recently, we have allowed ourselves to commit certain frivolities, thus many of us harnessed pack horses into wagons. That's what I did as well. Today my wagon did not arrive so I was left without dinner.

20 October [1 November]. Sunday.

We made a 60 *versta*s long march today, all in the same direction. Leaving at 4 am, we arrived late at night to Suleika, a village located on the road from Yukhnov to Gzhatsk. To my great delight, my wagon arrived – yesterday it simply got lost on the road. For several days the cold makes itself felt, [sometimes] it becomes unbearably cold. The courier from General Platov brought two flags taken from the enemy at Vyazma, and reported the capture of another 20 cannon.

21 October [2 November]. Monday.

The French retreat has [essentially] began after the battle at Maoyaroslavets. Moscow is free from the enemy. Now that we know which road they are moving on and considering that our corps is moving in the same direction as well, this is a whole epoch for my diary. It has been a while since our men received permission to cook soup, and today they were fortunate because we departed only at 10 o'clock in the morning. We again veered off the main road, which we reached yesterday, and moving by country road leading to Vyazma, we arrived at the village of Dubrovnaya (some 27 *versta*s [18 miles] from Vyazma) at 5 o'clock in the evening. Throughout the day we heard explosions of gunpowder caissons and, from time to time, cannonade. At nightfall, the Cossacks, famous for their night sorties, continue to attack the French. The enemy is retreating in the direction of Smolensk. It is said that a detachment of our troops is already near Smolensk, in which case it must anticipate the enemy there.

22 October [3 November]. Tuesday.

At 7 am gunfire erupted in the vanguard that was near Vyazma (the battle of Vyazma [has began]). We were told to be ready to fight, and yet, despite this order, we departed for Vyazma only 12 pm. By dusk, we made a small halt, and then continued on country roads in the same direction. The darkness and cold greatly complicate our campaign. We stopped only at 11 o'clock at night near the village of Bykovo, about eight *versta*s from Vyazma; we had to take up positions in the brushwood. This place is so uneven that one cannot find a place to sleep.

23 October [4 November]. Wednesday.

Standing still at the bivouac near Bykovo.

24 October [5 November]. Thursday.

We departed at 6:30 am and moved on country road parallel to the Vyazma-Smolensk main road. After marching for some 20 *versta*s in three and half hours, we halted at the village of Krasnoe.

25 October [6 November]. Friday.

We departed at 6:30 am and walked for 12 hours straight. Our corps stopped by the village of Gavryukovo. Snow and wind strongly interfered on march. Wanting to reach the bivouac earlier, I went ahead at a trot, but, unfortunately, not knowing the road, I got lost and found myself on the road where the 8th and 3rd Corps were moving. Consequently, I found myself in Gavryukovo just as my column entered it.

26 October [7 November]. Saturday.

After leaving at 8 am in the direction of Yelnya, we walked until dusk and stopped at Belyi Kholm, Despite the heavy snow, it is awfully cold. This is the most painful march that we had ever made, it is even worse than the one from Davgelishki [See June 18 entry].

27 October [8 November]. Sunday.

At Yelnya. As a duty officer, I went with a report to the general. Returning to our camp, I delivered to my comrades the most pleasant news that we could expect in our situation - a permission to sleep in apartments. By virtue of this order, at 10 pm, our corps entered Yelnya where it took up quarters. One can imagine how joyful we are after a 4-month stay in tents, not to mention extreme cold to which we were exposed.

28 October [9 November]. Monday.

A day of rest at Yelnya. I received a letter from St. Petersburg.

29 October [10 November]. Tuesday.

The corps departed at 8 am, heading from Yelnya to Smolensk. After 24 miles, we occupied quarters in the village of Balturino. Prior to our departure we received a report about the new brilliant victory that Platov secured over the enemy on the Dukhovschina road. He captured 62 guns and took 4,000 prisoners. We all are delighted with our victories, and when Prince Kutuzov was, as usual, passing by our columns, he was greeted and accompanied by mighty cheers which started spontaneously. Today we have seen plenty of prisoners who truly deserve our compassion. They are half-naked, some of them have told us that they have not eaten anything in the past 12 days. Complete exhaustion prevented them from going any further while the cruelty of the Cossacks, who escorted them, sometimes knew no bounds. I saw one of them who died of blood loss, and his comrade was lying next to him in this pool of blood, calmly awaiting death that would save him from suffering.

30 October [11 November]. Wednesday.

We again departed at 9 am. The main headquarters stopped at Lobkovo, located on the main road from Roslavl to Smolensk. Our corps was given quarters two *versta*s from the village of Grudino. We received plenty of joyful reports today. General [Mikhail] Miloradovich defeated the French at Smolensk and captured 150 guns, and 400 prisoners and 800 deserters. Then General Count Orlov destroyed a French cuirassier regiment and sent some 800 captured enemy cuirassiers to the commander in chief. Our three guerrillas – [Alexander] Seslavin, [Alexander] Figner and [Denis] Davydov – combined their forces to attack the warehouse of Napoleon's Imperial Guard and took 2,000 prisoners.

31 October [12 November]. Thursday.

A day of rest at Grudino. [The Life Guard] Finlyandskii Regiment was detached to attack the French who guarded a [mobile] magazine not far from our positions. The result of this excursion – the capture of the magazine and 400 prisoners, including 20 officers.

NOVEMBER

1 [13] November. Friday.

All battalions from our corps are on duty by turns at the headquarters of Prince Kutuzov. Today it was the turn of our battalion, so we went ahead of our division and proceeded to the village of Shelkanovo (a village on the road from Khislavichi to Smolensk), where the main headquarters was moved during the day. We had to squeeze together since all battalions officers had to stay in one room.

2 [14] November. Saturday.

Our division passed through Shelkanovo at 9 o'clock in the morning, our battalion joined it only for the duration of march and then proceeded to the village of Yurovo where Prince Kutuzov's headquarters was located. This village is situated between Shelkanovo and Krasnyi, where, in fact, we went next. Here we were again in the same cramped conditions as yesterday but I managed to stay with the orderlies of the commander-in-chief, who were fewer in numbers and had the best lodging. In the evening we had a feast, during which Okunev amused us to tears.

3 [15] November. Sunday.

A day of rest. I was thrilled to receive letters from my sisters and Madame B.

4 [16] November. Monday.

Camp at Novoselki, near Krasnyi. We marched with the entire division in complete order. It was very cold. We bivouacked about three *versta*s from Krasnyi where we are supposed to attack the enemy in the morning. In general, bivouac are very unappealing, especially after one spends some time in apartments, but, now, staying on the snow covered field under open sky seems particularly excruciating to us.

5 [17] November. Tuesday.

The attack began at dawn. Our two brigades were in reserves and, although they did not participate in the battle, spent the entire day under arms. The enemy corps, which fought at Krasnyi, were commanded by Marshal [Michel] Ney and Prince Eugene [de Beauharnais], they were cut off from the [main] French army and completely destroyed. In the evening I saw as men carried Colonel Grabovskii who was killed when he led the attack of his battalion of the Guard jagers. He was my sister's fiancé and a wonderful person; I was greatly upset by this occasion. At nightfall, our corps was deployed on the main road from Krasnyi to Orsha, about four or five *versta*s from Krasnyi. The position we occupied was almost entirely covered with corpses, and, to crown it all, our [supply] train, left at Novoselki, did not arrive so we had nothing to eat.

6 [18] November. Wednesday.

Standing still. Our cavalry was dispatched to pursue the enemy, who fled in all directions in confusion. Commander-in-Chief Prince Kutuzov arrived to our camp with a huge number of enemy flags. His face shone with happiness. He told us that between yesterday and the moment he spoke to us the enemy lost 152 guns while the number of prisoners is so high they have not been counted yet. There is nothing that could compare to universal joy that overwhelmed us at that moment and caused us to shed tears. The mighty "hurrah" cheer rang out and touched our old general.

7 [19] November. Thursday.

I was a duty officer in the division and, although we stayed in place, I had plenty of work; it was necessary to take precautions against the French deserters, wandering in the forests next to our camp. During the day we caught about 1,000 souls. It is believed that Marshal Ney's corps perished almost entirely. Already some 9,000 prisoners have been counted since the battle at Krasnyi.

8 [20] November. Friday.

Our corps departed at 8 o'clock in the morning, proceeding along country roads to Osha. The main headquarters went to Romanovo, near which we took up quarters in the village of Yushkino. This march was very exasperating due to poor roads from the thaw and rain.

9 [21] November. Saturday.

We marched again at 8 am. Prince Kutuzov's headquarters occupied the village of Savy, while we stayed at Krasnaya Slobodka. The weather was wonderful, and we actually enjoyed walking. We are just 25 miles from Orsha.

10 [22] November. Sunday.

A day of rest.

11 [23] November. Monday.

We departed at 8 o'clock in the direction of Kopys. Prince Kutuzov stopped at Morozovo, while we are at Pogulievo.

12 [24] November. Tuesday.

We marched two hours later than usual, that is, at 10 o'clock in the morning, and stopped with the main headquarters at Kopys. This is a small town on the main road from Orsha to Mogilev.

13 [25] November. Wednesday.

A day of rest. All of the Guard officers gathered at [the apartment of] Field Marshal Prince Kutuzov to accompany him into the church where a thanksgiving service for victory gained at Krasnyi and subsequent success was held. After lunch, I went, with a few friends, for a walk along the town's streets. Many prisoners, due to the lack of lodgings, are kept in large courtyards. Sp we went to look at them and saw firsthand that they surely deserve empathy. They were dying from hunger that recently completely wore them out. Unfortunately, we could not supply them with bread because we were deprived of it ourselves. We bought them a jug of vodka, and they nearly killed each other to get it. I had to restore order among them. I will never forget the sound of the voice with which one of the prisoners told me: "Messieurs, God will reward you." It is said that we already have more than 8,000 prisoners, which causes problems with supplies and provisions. Our soldiers treat prisoners remarkably cordially and share their meager portions with them. I oftentimes noticed as the soldiers of my company left their ranks as we marched to share their last biscuit with some unfortunate Frenchman freezing by the side of the road in the snow.

14 [26] November. Thursday.

We departed at 9 am. The crossing of the Dnieper in Kopys was extremely difficult because of very poor bridges. We had to cross them almost in single file and this took a long time. However, the march itself was relatively short. The main headquarters moved to Staroselye, a village on the road from Mogilev to Smolensl. We are housed in barracks near the headquarters. Grand Duke Constantin Pavlovich joined the army today. He again assumed the command of our corps, which is not particularly pleasant for us because pedantry will once again rule the day.

15 [27] November. Friday.

We left at 8 o'clock in the morning. The main headquarters occupied a small village of Krugloe while we took a nearby settlement. The Grand Duke, leading the cavalry, appeared in uniform only, without a coat, despite the bitter cold. He wanted to set an example, but we were getting chilled by just looking at him.

16 [28] November. Saturday.

Our division took quarters at Zaozerye. We arrived there only about 7 pm after a 12-hour trek. The weather was horrible: a strong wind, rain and cold. The entire regiment was billeted to three houses but, despite such confined conditions, we were thrilled to just have lodgings. The direction, in which we are proceeding now, is parallel to the road running from Orsha to Minsk.

17 [29] November. Sunday.

The division, departing at 8 am, occupied quarters in Belavichi. It was very cold, but because the road run through the woods, we were protected from the wind, so the cold was not as sharp as yesterday. In the morning we received unpleasant news that Napoleon, despite [the efforts of] Admiral Chichagov's army, managed to cross the Berezina, was thus safe and on the way to Vilna. However, another courier arrived later in the day reporting that the rear guard of the French Army was completely defeated by the armies of Admiral Chichagov and Count Wittgenstein at Borisov. Count Wittgenstein distinguished himself following a series of successful engagements with the enemy near Polotsk in early July, when he was detached from us. It would have been for him not to seek more victories but instead prevent Napoleon's escape. No one can explain why we did not anticipate Napoleon to the Berezina or did not appear there simultaneously with the French army. We are exhausted from so much marching with no gains to show for it. Yet, we suffered heavy losses from our marches and there is not a single company in the entire regiment that has more than 50 men under arms.

18 [30] November. Monday.

Standing still. Field Marshal's main headquarters moved forward to the Berezina.

19 November [1 December]. Tuesday.

We moved towards Oreshkovichi, this is the village on the left bank of the Berezina, downstream from Borisov.

20 November [2 December]. Wednesday.

Our division crossed the Berezina with great difficulties. We then proceeded in the same direction parallel to the main road from Borisov to Minsk, and took up quarters at Belichany.

21 November [3 December]. Thursday.

Standing still. Today is our regimental holiday.[27] In the absence of the Orthodox Church we he held a prayer in a kościół [Polish Catholic

---

[27] The Life Guard Semeyonovskii Regiment's regimental holiday was celebrated on 21 November, which also a major Christian holiday, the Presentation of the Blessed Virgin Mary (as it is known in the West), or The Entry of the Most Holy Theotokos into the Temple.

church] and then all dined at Colonel Posnikov's, who commanded the regiment after Kriedener's disgrace.

22 November [4 December]. Friday.

The division, continuing its advance, reached Klinniki. Field Marshal [Kutuzov] left us and hastened to Admiral Chichagov, who, after his exploits at the Berezina, pursued the French in the direction of Vilna.

23 November [5 December]. Saturday.

We made a 30-*versta* [20 miles] long march under a strong wind. I did not inquire about the name of the village where our regiment halted because not a single soul could be found in it when we arrived. In Smolevichi, we crossed the road running to Igumen while the main headquarters stopped at Deinarovka, the village not far from which our regiment took up quarters. This march was extremely tiring; the regiment has numerous stragglers while five men died.

24 November [6 December]. Sunday.

This march was as wearisome as yesterday's and the cold got stronger. We walked on country road, leaving Minsk to our right. We then took up quarters at Galitsy. There were 23 officers in one room, all without dinner because our supply train could not arrive on time due to bad roads. Soldiers are also without any of apartments and dinner. Today the loss in men was even worse than yesterday, and many froze to death.

25 November [7 December]. Monday.

A day of rest. My cousin Ivan [Nikolayevich Pushin] was promoted to an officer's rank and to be an officer's rank [ensign], appointed to the [Life Guard] Litovskii [Lithuanian] Regiment and arrived here yesterday. I was very pleased to see him, and he stayed with us overnight.

26 November [8 December]. Tuesday.

Feeling unwell due to fatigue, I could not go with the regiment. So at 1 o'clock at night I traveled ahead in the sleigh with brother Ivan and our quartermaster. It was terribly cold, so as we passed by a magnificent aristocratic manor, I could not resist from asking the hosts to shelter us for several hours. It was not yet 4 o'clock in the morning, and, naturally, no one expects guests at such impermissible hour. Fortunately for us, the lord was dead and his widow was sick, so the doctor and other family members were awake. We have well treated, a fire was started in the fireplace, and we were served tea, coffee and punch. In this pleasant refuge we stayed until 7 o'clock in the morning, then continued our journey and reached our regimental lodgings at Kolonitsy well ahead of our regiment. Here I bid farewell to my brother and he returned to his regiment.

27 November [9 December]. Wednesday.

The regiment advanced towards Oshmyany and stopped in Zatychino. Still sick, I sat in the sledge and arrived in Zatychino ahead of the regiment.

28 November [10 December]. Thursday.

The regiment stopped at Ershevichi. Like yesterday, I traveled in a sleigh.

29 November [11 December]. Friday.

The regiment halted at Sidorovka. I again traveled in a sleigh with quartermasters.

30 November [12 December]. Saturday.

I finally recovered and was on duty in the division. The cold made itself felt more strongly than ever. I delivered report to the general and suffered greatly from cold.

DECEMBER

1 [13] December. Sunday.

We departed at 8 am and, after moving by country road towards Oshmyany, we stopped at Novoselki. The 5th and 6th Corps, consisting of two Guard divisions and one cuirassier Division, received orders to proceed to Vilna and take up quarters there. The French were defeated at Smorgon where they lost 86 guns.

2 [14] December. Monday.

We were on the march from 8 am until 1 pm. We are now at quarters in Boruny. The 6th Corps occupied lodgings here prior to us. Rumors claim that Napoleon has left the army for Paris.

3 [15] December. Tuesday.

Our regiment passed Oshmyany in the direction of Vilna and stopped at the outskirts of the town, next to the main road from Oshmyany to Vilna. This march I traveled together with the quartermasters. About two *versta*s from Oshmyany, I had the opportunity to witness a terrible sight. Entire fields were completely strewn with corpses; without exaggerating, I can say that there were about twenty corpses per every square sazhen; all townships, villages, taverns are devastated and filled with sick and dying.

4 [16] December. Wednesday.

After passing through the town of Rukoini, our regiment stopped at the village of Dolgovlya, about 10 *versta*s from Vilna. It is terrible cold here. Once again I traveled with the quartermasters and again witnessed the same terrible scenes along the road. Our lodgings is very cold, and I barely got warm.

5 [17] December. Thursday.

We jubilantly entered Vilna in the afternoon. The march here was only 10 *versta*s long but bitter cold and the time spent waiting at the barrier before entering the town completely wore us out. We paraded in front of a field marshal, who was surrounded by people. The mighty cheers of "hurrah" resounded in the air, and our old general wept. As I passed him, he congratulated me with good quarters. I was very flattered by such attention. So we have finally reached the end of the campaign that will glorify us forever, our Motherland is safe now. Napoleon flees forlorn and his numerous army no longer exists. I received quarters at [the house of] a certain Kulikovskii, on appearance, a kind old man. A good clean bed was at my disposal, and I could not believe my luck. Good bed, good room, and the end of a campaign – it is just too much [of goodness all] at once.

6 [18] December. Friday.

Who would have believed that I slept worse last night than in the bivouacs and in the most awful quarters. I think the habit of sleeping in poor beds, rising early as well as elation [about the end of the war] – these are the causes of my insomnia. I got up at daybreak and began writing letters; the rest of the day I spent in bringing order to my wardrobe, which was in a desperate condition.

8 [20] December. Sunday.

Today our regiment began its guard duty and I was a duty officer. The Grand Duke attended the parade. Yesterday I saw a French prisoner in the *hauptwache* where he was attended by his 11-year-old son. The latter was a lovely boy, and his affection and love for his father, his courage in the hardship that he already experienced compelled me to pay attention to him. The boy was given a little bit of soup, and, as he had not eaten for several days, he was very grateful for the food. I invited him to stay with me, and although he was aware that he will be very comfortable [with me], he refused to accept it because he found it impossible to leave his father in condition that he was in.

11 [23] December. Wednesday.

The emperor had arrived in Vilna. The entire city went to see the parade. The pardoned Poles did their best to show their devotion.

12 [24] December. Thursday.

The Emperor's Birthday. In the evening the city was beautifully illuminated. The same decorations that were used during the festivities arranged by Napoleon were used now as well, but with some modifications, so as to replace the letter "N" with the letter "A," supplanting a single-headed French eagle with the Russian double-headed one. Apparently, the joy and rejoicing were universal. The Field Marshal organized a ball that ended at 4 o'clock in the morning. Two enemy's flags, which were very conveniently received from General Platov's advance guard just before the ball, were thrown under the feet of the Emperor as he entered the hall. His Majesty then awarded Prince Kutuzov with the Order of St. George (1st class). General [Yakov] Potemkin was appointed commander of our regiment.

14 [26] December. Saturday.

Our regiment held a parade. Since arriving the Emperor declared that he was upset at us because of the Kriedener affair. His Majesty ordered Colonel Posnikov come into his office for explanations.

15 [27] December. Sunday.

Count [Aleksei] Arakcheev's courier came to me with orders to appear in front of [Colonel Nikolai] Myakinin, the count's adjutant. So today I went to Myakinin, who handed me a letter from Madame B., from which I learned that she had met [Ober-procuror of the Holy Synod Ivan] Pukalov and, through him, she was able sway Count Arakcheyev in my favor. He promised her to grant me a courier trip to St. Petersburg. I asked Myakinin to introduce me to the Count, and he promised to do it tomorrow.

16 [28] December. Monday.

We were all summoned to Colonel Posnikov who informed us that the Emperor was very displeased with us and if he currently does not impose penalties on the main instigators, it was only thanks to the Grand Duke, to whom he promised this. In addition, by leaving the army, Colonel Kriedener had bound [the Emperor's hands] by such an unworthy and lowly act. Then the colonel told us that the emperor gave Colonel Pisarev a [regular] regiment so he could distinguish himself [on the field of battle] and justify in the Emperor's eyes clemency extended to him by His Majesty. Colonel Vladimir Nabokov replaced Pisarev as our battalion commander. Leaving Colonel Posnikov we went to introduce ourselves to our new regimental commander, General Potemkin, and from there I went to meet Count Arakcheyev, who was very busy and could not receive me, so my introduction was delayed for another day. During his conversation with Colonel Posnikov, the Emperor said: "Fedor Nikolayevich, I would have cared not that this is the regiment of Peter the Great himself and would have disbanded it at once, but my hands are tied by the request of the Grand Duke and the behavior of Kriedener. You have to serve hard and long before you will make me forget what had happened."

18 [30] December. Wednesday.

Today Count Arakcheev has finally received me, and quite warmly, but he also firmly told me that while the Emperor and the Grand Duke are here, he cannot send me as courier anywhere. My brother Nicholas has recovered from the wound he sustained and arrived in Vilna today.

19 [31] December. Thursday.

We were told to be prepared to march out at the first order.

20 December [1 January 1813]. Friday.

We buried Lieutenant [Yegor] Wedemeyer.[28] He is the second officer we have lost in Vilna. [Lieutenant Mikhail] Osipov was the first. These gentlemen, who were spared by enemy bullets and cold, could not survive the pestilence in Vilna.

21 December [2 January]. Saturday.

Buinevich, the one with whom I shared lodgings at Matskovichi, visited me today. He was pleased to find me seeing me safe and sound.

23 December [4 January]. Monday.

We are scheduled to depart tomorrow. Our quartermasters left today.

24 December [5 January]. Tuesday.

We stayed under arms since 7 am. The Emperor reviewed us at Pogulianka and, at 11 o'clock in the morning, we left Vilna. We marched to the town of Gobot and stopped at Sviotniki, not far from that town. [However] our third brigade, jagers and the [Life Guard] Finlyandskii Regiment returned to Vilna after the review.

25 December [6 January]. Wednesday.

Each regiment departed separately today. Our regiment left at 7 am and made a rather long march. Our battalion, passing through Leipuni, stopped in the village of Zahara.

26 December [7 January]. Thursday.

A day of rest at Zahara.

---

[28] Wedemeyer was only 22 years old.

27 December [8 January]. Friday.

We left at 7 o'clock in the morning. The headquarters of General Lavrov went to Kamen'. Our battalion proceeded to Orany place and took quarters at Okolitsa-Talkuni. As a duty officer, I, before going to my lodgings, first appeared with a report in front of General Lavrov, and as usual, he instructed me to convey his order to the [Life Guard] Prebrazhenskii Regiment. Knowing well that he forgets half of his orders after issuing them and understanding that the order he gave me was completely pointless and futile and that, probably, it would be cancelled before I reached the regiment, I decided not to trouble myself with going to the Preobrazhenskii Regiment and instead went straight to Okolitsa-Talkuni, traveling through the woods that separated the village from Orany. I made a right decision because [had I went to the regiment] the nightfall would have caught me in the woods, where I would have been lost without bringing any benefit to anyone.

28 December [9 January]. Saturday.

At Merech, a town on the banks of the Niemen. Departing at 9 o'clock in the morning [from Okolitsa-Talkuni], we reached Merech before the Emperor who arrived by noon. We are finally on the border where only the Nieman River separates us from the Duchy of Warsaw.

30 December [11 January]. Monday.

[Two] platoons from our regiment and the Preobrazhenskii Regiment were selected to carry out the execution of Cornet Nezhinskii of the Gorodetskii Dragoons Regiment, who was court-martialed for defecting to the enemy and sentenced to death. A young man of Polish origin, he deliberately fell behind during our retreat and defected to the French, but was taken prisoner by the Cossacks in Vilna. The capital sentence was carried out at 10 o'clock. This incident kept me upset for the rest of the day.

31 December [12 January]. Tuesday.

We received order to depart tomorrow. Our quartermasters have left today. We are about to cross the border.

THE 1813 CAMPAIGN

JANUARY

1 [13] January. Wednesday.

Early in the morning we gathered on the banks of the Neman River, where we held a solemn farewell prayer. The enemy was longer within the Russian realm. Our battalions descended on the steep banks of the river and crossed to the other side under the sounds of drum beating and a military march. It was truly a solemn moment. This is the first step toward the challenge posed by Europe. Each battalion climbed on the left bank of the river, shouting "Hurrah." The enthusiasm was general. After crossing the Neman, we entered the Duchy of Warsaw.

Imperial quarters occupied Leipuny, a small town, which we passed to occupy quarters in Vilkonis. This was a long march but no one complained of fatigue. Each of us was pleased to take the battle away from our country.

2 [14] January. Thursday.

We again made a long march, and stopped at the village of Stobinki, not far from the town of Sejny, where I encountered an innkeeper, a 96 years old Prussian who well remembered the Seven Years War.

For last few years the Duchy of Warsaw has been part of the Confederation of the Rhine and ruled by the Saxon King [Frederick Augustus I]. An old countryman assured me that they have lived better under the Prussian rule and, in particular, he complained of the taxes and conscription.

3 [15] January. Friday.

Our regiment, deployed in various villages for the night, gathered at Sejny and made a short trek along the Krasnopol road. I took up quarters not far from the village of Stabelszizna. In Sejny, we found a tavern where we had a very good dinner. It was quite a surprise for us since we are accustomed to seeing everything devastated and ruined on our path, like it was on the road to Vilna. As soon as I reached Stabelszizna, a detachment of the Horse Guards under the command of Kablukov[29] also arrived there. Perhaps it was mistakenly sent to the village already occupied by us, but we now have to squeeze in together until new orders arrive.

4 [16] January. Saturday.

A day of rest, but not for the Horse Guards; they were transferred to another village.

5 [17] January. Sunday.

We marched out by battalions. Our battalion departed at 8 am and, passing towns of Krasnopol and Suwalki, it stopped in Krapivna. It is bitterly cold here. Luckily for us, the terrain here is rolling and covered with forests which protect us from winds.

Suwalki is a beautiful place; the Imperial Quarters is located here since yesterday. His Majesty was standing at the window and watching as we passed by. It was said that the Emperor would stay here a few days.

6 [18] January. Monday.

We departed by battalions and occupied quarters at Vranovo, after passing the township of Raczki. Despite the bitter cold, all Jews in Raczki rode out on horseback to meet the Emperor. They bore a canopy that was entirely gilded, bread and many valuable gifts.

Our current position is only half a *versta* away from the Prussian border. One can recognize this without looking at a map, but simply observing buildings. Every house has an oven with chimney, earthenware crockery is of German style, customs and manners of the inhabitants are more Prussian than Polish. The population seems more favorably disposed to us and is incomparably more generous to us than the French.

7 [19] November. Tuesday.

We left at 8 am, and, by 9 o'clock, we were already in Prussia. The Imperial quarters went to Kalinowo, while we moved a bit further to the village of Skamenta [today Mazurovo]. This place formerly belonged to the *mazurs*.[30] The population speaks a dialect of mixed Polish and German. Manners and clothing are all Prussian. Our tavern-keeper

---

[29] Colonel Platon Kablukov commanded a squadron in the Horse Guard Regiment

[30] Mazur refers to the Protestant population of the northwestern Poland.

assured me he did not remember such a severe winter as this. Indeed, the cold was terrible, and yet there was very little snow on the fields.

8 [20] January. Wednesday.

The Imperial Quarters stopped at Łęk [Elk], a very beautiful place. Here we camped as well, finding a very decent tavern which is a very important on the campaign. We took up lodgings about half a *versta* from Łęk, at the village of Muncza. The cold is not as strong today, but it still is very unpleasant to go out of a warm room to deliver a report to General Lavrov; today I was a duty officer. Notwithstanding the cold I delivered my report, and thence went to the divisional headquarters at Barany.

9 [21] January. Thursday.

A day of rest at Muncza. In the morning I went to Pisarev and we travelled together to Łęk to meet Count Arakcheyev who received us very well. I handed the count's adjutant my letter to Madame B. and my diary describing my experiences up to date. I promised to Madame B. to send it and today I fulfilled this promise.

10 [22] January. Friday.

We marched for 4 *versta*s today. The Imperial quarters at Drygaly while we are a little farther at the village of Kruszewo. The 8th and 9th Companies took common quarters. When we passed through Drygaly, local residents came out to greet the Emperor, who welcomed them, as elsewhere, with clear delight.

11 [23] January. Saturday.

The Imperial quarters moved to Johanesburg. Our battalion went one *versta* [0.6 mile] further to the village of Mittel-Pogobin. Leaving Kruszewo, we stopped for a short time in Biala, a small town where we still managed to get something for breakfast. The road from Johanesburg to Mittel-Pogobin passes through vast pine woods that are known as the Royal Forest.

12 [24] January. Sunday.

A day of rest. Our battalion has to take a turn guarding the Imperial quarters and I, as a duty officer, lead it to Johanesburg. Usually the changing of the guard took place without a formal ceremony but today the Emperor desired to attend it and since we were not prepared for it, he was quite displeased.

I spent the day in the tavern because there was no other place to stay. In the evening an illumination was arranged. In front of the windows of the Emperor a pyramid was erected with a banner that was inscribed: "Glory to Alexander the Great Liberator of Europe."

The people filled the entire street and cheers to Russia never ceased. At this time the Emperor, not paying attention to the rapturous welcome by the Prussians, locked in his apartment with several musicians from the Preobrazhenskii and Semeyonovskii Regiments and rehearsed with them the mass which, according to his wishes, will be held tomorrow. This rehearsal lasted a long time, and I could rest only at 1 am.

13 [25] January. Monday.

The Emperor again came to observe the changing of the guard. Noticing that my people were without knapsacks, he became angry at me, gave me a reprimand and ordered me to be placed for 24 hours under arrest. This reprimand, though not strict, upset me very much because it was imposed not so much for my service faults but rather due to the Kriedener affair in which I played the same role as the rest of my comrades. I relinquished my command to the next senior officer after me and ordered him to go to Kurvienu, where our regiment was supposed to arrive during the day. I, meanwhile, went personally to Count Arakcheyev, who sent for me. He was present at the scene between the Emperor and me and told me that His Majesty told him that he long knew me as a good officer but found it necessary to punish me for my absent-mindedness. After this explanation I left Johanesburg, which the Imperial quarters was not yet planning to leave, and went to the headquarters of General Potemkin at Kurvienu, and, from there, rejoined my company at Gaidyn where I served the arrest in my quarters.

14 [26] January. Tuesday.

The Imperial quarters transferred to Friedrichsdorf, and our regiment moved one *versta* farther to Kabbasi. While under arrest, I did not go with the regiment but separately from it. In the evening I got my sword back.

15 [27] January. Wednesday.

The Imperial quarters moved to Willenberg while we halted two *versta*s away from it at Rakownice. The Emperor was standing at the window when we passed through Willenberg and the entire population of the town, which blocked the street, was awed while gazing at us. The Moscow campaign made us famous all over Europe. The room, where we were billeted, was not as cramped as usual and, in addition, we received orders to take quarters in a few more villages that we find available. We probably did not stop here just for one day.

16 [28] January. Thursday.

Count Arakcheyev sent a note that I should see him in Willenberg; therefore, not knowing how much downtime we had, I went at once. The count wanted to see me only to give me a letter from Madame B. and take my letters to her. He took it upon himself to deliver my love letters. I soon returned from Willenberg and, since in my absence, one more available village of Przidun or Sutzen Hofen was located, I was ordered to go there with the 8th and 9th Companies. I deployed them there and then spent the night at Rakownice that is located nearby.

17 [29] January. Friday.

In the morning I went with my officers from Rakownice to Przidun. I must note that my roommates had all changed by now. I am now quartering with the officers of 8th Company, where my friends are M. Brinken, brothers [Pavel and Nikolai] Khrapovitskii and both [Platon and Vasilii] Raczinskis. Zotov was also in our company but stayed behind because of illness. Prince Dadiani became an officer and was transferred to one of the regular regiments while Princes Trubetskoy had fallen behind our regiment for a long time already. No sooner had we settled in Przidun that our Quartermaster Nikolai Khrapovitskii was called up and, upon returning, he told us that we will depart tomorrow.

18 [30] January. Saturday.

We marched in the direction of Janowo but, before reaching this place, the corps headquarters and our regimental headquarters stopped at Roczen. We are again on the border of Prussia and the Duchy of Warsaw. The Royal Forest ends at Willenberg so we found ourselves in an open area. The cold made itself felt strongly. I froze my nose and was advised to rub it till blood comes out which caused me unbearable pain.

19 [31] January. Sunday.

We made a very long march today. At the village of Janowo we crossed the border and entered the Duchy of Warsaw. The corps headquarters occupied Uniszki-Zawadskie while I, with the 8th and 9th Companies, stopped at Studence, a village not far from Mlawa. As the duty officer I had to deliver report but I was so overcome with laziness that I did not do it. It was claimed that the inhabitants of the Duchy [of Warsaw] have risen up against us and count some 60 thousand people, armed mostly with axes.

20 January [1 February]. Monday.

A day of rest. We received ordered to keep our eyes open and take precautions against the local population, which, it was feared, might rebel. Therefore, we had to deploy sentries, even though our poor soldiers were exhausted with fatigue.

21 January [2 February]. Tuesday.

We marched for about three *versta*s. The corps headquarters went to Wroblewo while our battalion, together with the 2nd Battalion, proceeded to Linsen.

22 January [3 February]. Wednesday.

Another light march. The Horse Guards occupied quarters so close to us that they completely constrained us. We stopped at Ciesle, just before the town of Drobin. Our lodgings are insufferably disgusting.

Some of our officers congratulated me assuring that I was promoted to colonel but since the order of the day was not received yet, I could not bring myself to believe this news.[31]

23 January [4 February]. Thursday.

A day of rest. We settled down so miserably that are not even satisfied with a day's rest. The difference between this country and Prussia is very noticeable. In this damned Duchy we are deprived of basic necessities and even a shoddy wooden bed cannot be obtained without a lot of trouble. Tables are a rarity. The rooms are so low that even I, despite my small stature, kept constantly hitting my head against the ceiling.

---

[31] The order promoting Pushin to a colonel was indeed approved on 22 January 1813.

We think that we will next go to Plock. Our men are completely exhausted. Many of them are sick and, even if you combine all three battalions, their numbers would only match that of a single full-roster company. Upon leaving St. Petersburg, the 9th Company, which I commanded, comprised of 4 officers, 16 NCOs and 165 privates (a full roster). And yet, when we entered Vilna, I was the only one present from among officers, followed by two non-commissioned officers and 22 privates. All other companies were in the same condition so that all 12 companies, which made up the regiment, could hardly muster up to 300 men. Such a huge loss in human lives occurred largely because of exhaustion, cold and disease, not enemy bullets or gunfire.

24 January [5 February]. Friday.

Today's march was not long but the wind caused us plenty of trouble. The corps headquarters headed for Dombrowsk, and our regiment to Klinow. We were given such small lodgings there that they could hold only officers so soldiers had to stay in the backyards.

25 January [6 February]. Saturday.

At Plock. We entered the town by a parade march but in such small numbers that we were laughable. Nevertheless, the Emperor himself led us into the town. Unfortunately, our regiment took its turn of guarding the Imperial quarters the day before so not all units of the regiment managed to take their places in the ranks on time, as a result we had tussle around to line up. We managed to somehow gather six small units that we combined into one battalion, although a rather small one. The Preobrazhenskii and Semeyonovskii Regiments took up quarters inside Plock itself while other units were billeted in the suburbs.

Illumination was staged in the evening.

The prefect of the city went in person to greet the Emperor at the gates of the city. During my lunch in a restaurant, I saw a Pole who was overjoyed by the courteous reception he received from our Monarch. He told the tavern keeper that he was not hungry and that he did not even want to think about food after the honor that was bestowed upon him by His Majesty, who honored him with a conversation. I could not resist telling this eccentric, that if the Emperor continues to pay him attention, he might die of starvation.

26 January [7 February]. Sunday.

The next morning I paid a visit to Count Arakcheyev and, in the evening, attended a theater, which turned out to be a rather poor one.

27 January [8 February]. Monday.

General Potemkin told me that I can wear a colonel's epaulettes, even though the order of the day [announcing my promotion] has not yet reached the regiment. My joy was boundless.

28 January [9 February]. Tuesday.

Wanting to share my happiness with my loved ones, I went to show my colonel's epaulettes to my cousins Nikolai and Ivan, who were deployed in a village, some three *versta*s from the city. They too were delighted by my promotion and we parted only by late evening. The village, where my brothers were quartered, is a Prussian colony: the road leading them from Plock runs through a wonderful countryside. I admired everything around me and was in a state of rapture. Some place seemed prettier to me than they were in reality. In general, this day gave me so many good memories, and let's hope that such days occur more often in our lives.

29 January [10 February]. Wednesday.

Warsaw and Pulawy were captured three days ago.[32] These news, received this morning together with a report about two victories gained near Danzig,[33] greatly delighted us and as soon as the emperor appeared at the parade, we greeted him with incessant cheers. Then, when His Majesty was returning home after the parade surrounded by nearly all the officers, old field marshal [Mikhail Kutuzov] appeared as well and all of a sudden everyone, including the Emperor, burst with a mighty cheer. It was a wonderful moment of common enthusiasm that was sincere and spontaneous.

Later that day I went to dine with [Mikhail] Arsenyev, the commander of the guard cavalry[34] that was deployed about one *versta* from Plock, in the village of Wladywa, on the road by which we arrived at Plock. I was

---

[32] Miloradovich occupied Warsaw on 7 February while Wittgenstein took Pulawy (Pillau) the following day.

[33] Pushin refers to Lieutenant General Lowis' operations to blockade Danzig.

[34] Arsenyev also commanded the Life Guard Horse Regiment.

accompanied by [Staff] Captain [Nikolai] Stürler. We both liked our walk so much that decided to take it more often, and as soon as opportunity and possibility present themselves. But the Fate itself desired this to be our last trip because as soon as we went to bed we received order to make an unexpected departure in the morning, which dashed our dreams.[35]

30 January [11 February]. Thursday.

We left Plock at 8 am. Although the Vistula was still frozen, the ice was weak. We crossed it safely. After moving to the left bank, we marched to Blümfelberg, a Prussian colony about 3 *versta*s from Plock and two *versta*s from Gombin. The corps headquarters went to Nowy Weski while the Imperial quarters remained in Plock.

31 January [12 February]. Friday – 1 [13] February. Saturday.

We are standing still.

FEBRUARY

2 [14] February. Sunday.

The Emperor left Plock, but we passed through Gostynin on the way to Lanieta, where the main headquarters was located. We took quarters at Jastrzebia.

3 [15] February. Monday.

The Imperial quarters moved to Klodawa, the corps headquarters to Dzerbice, while we halted at a landlord's estate in Chodowo.

---

[35] Pushin later added the following note: "Captain Stürler, who soon promoted to colonel and appointed commander of the Leib-Grenadier Regiment in our corps, was a Swiss native. He entered the Russian service before the 1812 Campaign. A blue-blooded aristocrat, he hated the French. He was accepted [into the Russian service] as a lieutenant in the Semeyonovskii Regiment and we became very close friends. He was a very brave officer; wounded at Pirna, he claimed that he took notice of the sharpshooter who shot him so wishing to avenge himself he got his wound dressed and returned to frontline but was wounded again and forced to leave. Upon my promotion to a colonel he took over the command of my 9th Company. He learned Russian language but spoke inaccurately which amused us... He was killed in 1825 during the uprising of December 14." Stürler was shot by the Decembrist P. Kakhovskii on the Senate Square during the Decembrist Uprising on 26 December 1825.

4 [16] February. Tuesday.

A day of rest.

5 [17] February. Wednesday.

The Imperial quarters moved to Kolo while we stopped at Chojny, about one *versta* from the town. Local Jews, dressed in clothes similar to the Turkish costumes, came out on horseback to greet the Emperor.

6 [18] February. Thursday.

A day of rest. I went to Count Arakcheyev to mail, through him, a letter but I learned in Kolo that he is with the Emperor about half a *versta* from town. So I sent the letter, and returned to Chojny without meeting the kind count.

7 [19] February. Friday.

The Imperial quarters moved to Konin while we are at Brizen-Holender. The word "*holender*" is added to the name of each Prussian colony - it comes from the word "*holen*," meaning cut out of wood, and refers to colonists clearing the forest to inhabit the area that is entirely covered with trees. All the colonists live much better than the Poles and are incomparably richer than them.

8 [20] February. Saturday.

Standing still. I went to Konin to see Count Arakcheyev but now, like the last time, he was with the Emperor at some distance from town, so I spent time looking around this place. Konin is a small village, beautifully situated on the island of the river Warta, and from a distance it gives the impression of a large and beautiful city. The highest point is occupied by the ruins of the castle of King Boleslaw[36]. I could not climb there on my horse but, having another companion, a fellow enthusiast of climbing, we both went up this mountain and reached its top, where there were ruins. From there we enjoyed a wonderful sight that opened to us when the Emperor, surrounded by a vast retinue, drove into town, proceeded to the headquarters of Field Marshal Prince [Kutuzov] and entered inside it. The

---

[36] King of Poland who died in 1081.

crowd, carrying icons, rushed to meet the Emperor and grouped in the streets near the house of the old general.

I did not regret what I had seen, and returned very pleased to Brizen-Holender, despite not having fulfilled my wish of meeting Count Arakcheyev. The spring is in the air and walking brings so much pleasure.

Today we received a report of the victory gained by Count Wittgenstein three *versta*s outside Berlin.

9 [21] February. Sunday.

Standing still. I again took a brief walk in Konin. The Emperor attended the Te Deum held on the occasion of the victory near Berlin. It is said that our troops have already occupied this capital. King of Prussia [Frederick William III] is in Breslau, and Austrian [Emperor Francis Joseph] departed without announcing whether he is out ally or not.

10 [22] February. Monday.

We made a short march of two *versta*s and stopped at Tulickowe.

11 [23] February. Tuesday.

Departing at 8 am, we stopped at rather meager quarters in Piątrozol.

12 [24] February. Wednesday.

All of the Imperial Guard gathered at the Kalisz gate, waiting for arrival of the emperor. The Jews, as usual, gathered in their strange attire to greet the victorious monarch, to whom they wished to express their sincere devotion.

Finally the emperor arrived, stopped ahead of us and, with banners flying and drums beating, we solemnly entered the city, which was in French hands just 8 days ago. After passing Kalish from one end to another, I moved for another *versta* out of town and took an apartment in the house of the owner of the village in Węngry. The Imperial quarters and the main headquarters of Field Marshal [Kutuzov] remained in Kalisz.

13 [25] February. Thursday.

I went to Kalisz on my personal business. Paid a visit to Count Arakcheyev, who gave me a letter [from Madame B] and took my letters.

The rest of the day I was inspecting the city. It is located very close to the Prussian border and is quite attractive. There are several two-storey houses, a boulevard and numerous water wells in the streets. It is believed that the King of Prussia will arrive to meet our sovereign, therefore, people expect that this will be a long halt. I returned to Węngry for the night.

14 [26] February. Friday.

Today it was our regiment's turn to guard [Imperial quarters] and as a duty officer in charge of the guard I went to Kalisz for 24 hours. I dined with the commandant of the palace, and spent the night with [Vasili] Bakunin [Sub-Lieutenant of the Leib-Grenadier Regiment].

15 [27] February. Saturday.

After changing of the guard, I went to see General Potemkin, who had a lunch with him.

Returning to Węngry, I met my landlord who lives nearby and paid a visit to me. He asked me to honor him with my visit.

16 [28] February. Sunday.

The Emperor rewarded us with a six-month pay so I went to get my salary at the regimental headquarters located in a village where General Potemkin was billeted. Then I went to Kalisz with the intention of attending a mass in a church, but Count Arakcheyev kept me for too long and I was late to church. In the evening there was a ball that ended quite late so I stayed with Bakunin.

17 February [1 March]. Monday.

Count Timon treated us to breakfast, so I could not get out of Kalisz before 2 pm. Returning to Węngry, I found [my cousin] Ivan [Pushin] who stayed for the night at my place.

18 February [2 March]. Tuesday.

In the village of Węngry, in addition to the house which we shared with the landlord, there was another house that was completely empty. So we decided to move there. This had to be done because of our comrade's Pavel Khrapovitskii's serious illness; he needed a rest and our presence perturbed him. We left him in this quarters, and moved over to the new one.

I cannot but comment on the disease of Khrapovitskii, our poor lad. On the 8th, at Brizen-Holender, he was still feeling himself quite well and even said that it was impossible for a person to die suddenly because every person, who takes care of himself, will certainly feel the approach of death; he was even ready to bet that would live another few days. To which I jokingly remarked that I can hardly keep his bet because he was about to die tomorrow. As I finished my sentence, Brinken sneezed - it is a well known Russian belief that anything said is true if someone sneezes at that moment. We all laughed, assuring Khrapovitskii that he would die tomorrow. He laughed as well but the next day he fell ill and cannot recover since then. His illness is very serious.

19 February [3 March]. Wednesday.

Brinken dined with me and my brothers in Skalmierzyce.

20 February [4 March]. Thursday.

During the day I was in Kalisz, and in the evening - at a ball at General Potemkin's quarters.

21 February [5 March]. Friday.

We were invited to dine with the owner of the estate of Węgry at Kakowo. From there I went to visit Kostamarov. The Pole, with whom he lived, never ceased complaining about the damage and harassment that [Denis] Davydov's partisans caused him while passing through his possessions. I remarked to him that our advance guard had not yet received the order countermanding the former one that declared the residents [of the Duchy of Warsaw] as the inhabitants of countries hostile to us so he could not ask that our troops, in the midst of pursuing enemy forces, avoid taking whatever they needed, especially since the French, the Polish allies, treated them no better. The Pole indeed acknowledged that the French did not spare them but that the Poles had the right to expect and hope for a completely different treatment from the troops of Emperor Alexander, who is famous for his noble and generous character. Our dispute continued for a long time and ended with the Pole professing friendship and loyalty to us. I knew better what to believe.

22 February [6 March]. Saturday.

Despite the invitation I received from the jagers, three *versta*s long distance and bad weather forced me to give up on visiting them. I went to Count Arakcheyev to give him a letter addressed to Madame B., then had a dinner with [Yegor] Fuchs[37] and, not wishing to stay at a nobleman's ball, I returned to Węgry.

The weather was horrible, strong winds and hail forced me to close eyes. The driver lost his way, and I returned home completely wet, chilled and very late. Now what would have happened to me if I went to the jagers' party and were forced to travel 6 *versta*s, that is, three *versta*s to and from.

Zotov has recovered and rejoined us.

23 February [7 March]. Sunday.

Pavel Khrapovitskii has died. This is the same Khrapovitskii who caused the incident with Kriedener who told him, "You are walking like a doll in front of your platoon." Although Khrapovitskii, fearing consequences for his actions, tried to distract our officers from this incident, their patience [with Kriedener] was already worn out and they were only waiting for a chance to rebel.

My unfortunate prediction has come true. Maybe I should really become superstitious…

Field Marshal gave a ball in Kalisz, to which I received an invitation but did not want to leave Nikolai Khrapovitskii alone just after his brother has passed away. So I stayed with him.

As you can see it is our small band's destiny to not exceed six members - yesterday died Khrapovitskii, today arrived Zotov.

24 February [8 March]. Monday.

I had to attend the parade in Kalisz, but I was late and got annoyed for making a pointless journey in murderously atrocious [*ubiistvenno skvernaya*] weather.

---

[37] Head of Kutuzov's campaign chancellery.

27 February [11 March]. Thursday.

Our unfortunate comrade's funeral took place today. He was buried in Skalmierzyce. After the funeral, I stayed to dine with my cousins who were lodged in the same village, and returned to Węngry only in the evening. The elder Khrapovitskii, who is [a captain] in the Horse Guards, was very dejected.

MARCH

1 [13] March. Saturday.

I was in Kalisz, where he received, through Count Arakcheyev, a letter from Madame B. that upset me. She had questioned my affection for her, thought that I had forgotten her and reproached me I suspect that someone spoke badly about me to her.

2 [14] March. Sunday.

I attended a mass at the court church. Yesterday His Majesty received a communion, and attended the service today as well. In the evening he plans to travel to Breslau, where the Prussian king currently is.

Fuchs, with whom I dined today, frankly told me that he does not justify our Emperor paying a visit to the king, and instead thought it necessary for him to stay and wait in Kalisz. I disagreed with his view because, I reasoned, even if this move hurts the sovereign's vanity, it actually, in my opinion, carries an even greater value because we need an alliance with the Prussian king. His Majesty the King of Prussia has over 150 thousand men under arms, and we, in our current position, cannot refuse them. Our numbers are very scarce and we have lost more men from marching and diseases than in combat.

Thus conversing about politics, Fuchs and I strolled along the boulevards in Kalisz, which are very well maintained. They all run into the river Prosna, where they branch out, with one outlet running along the right bank, and the other on the left. The Prosna River flows into the Vartu about 15 *versta*s north-east from Kalisz. Kalisz, like Vilna, is surrounded by hills and is only visible from close distance.

7 [19] March. Friday.

We celebrated St. Joseph's day in Kalisz – it is a town festival. I was present at a mass in a kościół [Polish Catholic church]. Later I spent some time with Ivan, who was in Kalisz. The Emperor has returned from his trip to Breslau by 9 pm.

9 [21] March. Sunday.

My sister sent me letter regarding her apartment and asked me to discuss this issue with Count [Nikolai] Tolstoy, the head of the Imperial quarters. Early in the morning I went to Kalisz to complete my sister's request, but His Excellency [Tolstoy] told me that he had no time to read the letter and told me to come later for his answer. I attended a church service where the Emperor was as well. After the service, I returned to Count Tolstoy, but he again had no time for me. God knows what kind of person is he? He needs entire century to read just a few lines. Anyway, I decided to give him 24 hours, maybe during this time, he will do something.

Count Arakcheyev told me that the Prussian king greeted our Emperor two *versta*s [1.5 mile] from Breslau. All of the Prussian troops were under arms, and the incalculable crowds rushed to meet His Majesty, incessantly shouting "Long live Alexander! Long live our savior! Hurrah!" Despite his short stay in Breslau, the Emperor still found time to attend a play and a ball, and, the following morning, a parade as well.

10 [22] March. Monday.

There is a military school in Kalisz: I had the opportunity to see many young people, students from this school, under arms at the funeral of one of their comrade. They are very slim, dressed in the French model blue uniform with red lapels [*otvorot*] and wide trousers. Their weapons are proportional to their height and they carry them gracefully. The non-commissioned officers are given epaulettes: the senior NCOs have silver ones, and the junior - wool.

11 [23] March. Tuesday.

Finally, Count Tolstoy has deigned to give me answer, and satisfactory at that, and promised to write to Count [Senator Nikolai] Golovin in St. Petersburg so that after his marriage to the young lady [Sofia] de Ribas,[38]

---

[38] Pushin's sister, Elizabeth, and Sofia de Ribas were both ladies-in-waiting to Empress Elizabeth Alekseevna.

her rooms are set aside for my sisters. This was all we could have asked him to do so I'm very happy for my sisters.

Upon emerging from Count Tolstoy, I quickly had a dinner and then went to training. The rest of the day I spent at Count Potemkin's.

12 [24] March. Wednesday.

We took up the guard duty in Kalisz and conducted training in the presence of the Emperor. His Majesty was very pleased with us and told us that now we forgave us all for wronging Kriedener. Indeed, in Vilna, the Emperor declared that we had to work hard to earn his forgiveness, and back then we, being so miserable, thought that we would have to fight fiercely against the enemy to achieve this forgiveness, completely misunderstanding that a single successful training will replace at least one victory. The proof - that the battle of Borodino and the whole of immortal campaign in 1812 could not dispose His Majesty towards us as much as a single parade in Kalisz did.

The courier brought a report that Hamburg is occupied by our troops.

15 [27] March. Saturday.

Since Thursday, I suffer from a terrible toothache;[39] it is a bit better today which is very timely since we have been ordered to move up to Kalish and prepare for the arrival of the Prussian king, who is expected by the 18th.

16 [28] March. Sunday.

Our village of Węgry is very close to Kalisz, and since it was not needed to any corps that were approaching Kalisz under yesterday's order, we were thrilled to remain in our apartments.

17 [29] March. Monday.

The swelling of my cheek has almost entirely subsided which allowed me to go out. I went to Kalisz, and then dined with General Potemkin at

---

[39] Pushin suffered from periostitis, a medical condition caused by inflammation of the periosteum, a layer of connective tissue that surrounds bone, frequently of a jaw bone. The condition is generally chronic, and is marked by tenderness and swelling of the bone and an aching pain.

Smelowo. The weather was wonderful, and the spring air that I breathed during my trip, was very beneficial to me.

Our parade, scheduled for the 18th, was canceled and rescheduled for the 21st. The King of Prussia cannot come to Kalisz before the specified date, he is still in Berlin and we will be informed when he will return to Breslau.

18 [30] March. Tuesday.

I visited my brothers in Skalmierzyce.

21 March [2 April]. Friday.

We remained under arms since 9 o'clock in the morning. The troops lined up along the Breslau road in three lines and formed in a battle array. The right flank rested in Kalisz. The Emperor rode past us in a carriage, accompanied by a *sotnya* of the Black Sea Cossacks. We waited for his return until 4 p.m. in a rather strong heat. Finally he appeared with the Prussian king. They mounted their horses and moved by our troops accompanied by their numerous staff. As they approached, each battalion saluted, played a greeting tune and shouted "Hurrah." Afterwards they went to the town square while the troops paraded in front of them.

When it was all over, I was exhausted from fatigue. Knowing that tomorrow is our regiment's turn for guard duty and I would have to be to Kalisz, I decided to stay the night with Bakunin. In the evening, the city was illuminated, but the illumination was not anything outstanding.

22 March [3 April]. Saturday.

The Emperor and the King attended trainings and parade. I was a duty officer in charge of sentries. All senior officers of the Guard were presented to the King by the Emperor himself. In the evening Field Marshal Prince [Kutuzov] held a ball on behalf of a certain Countess Radulinski which was attended by the Emperor and the King until 11 o'clock. After dinner, I returned to Bakunin's place.

23 March [4 April]. Sunday.

Before the parade, the Emperor and King attended the training of the Cavalry Guard Regiment, while in the meantime I paid a visit to Count Arakcheyev. After the parade, I returned to Węgry, where I have not been in two days. My cheek is swollen again, apparently I got out too early.

24 March [5 April]. Monday.

The King of Prussia left Kalisz. I sat at home all day long, hoping for quick recovery.

25 March [6 April]. Tuesday.

Appointed as a chairman of the court-martial, I had to handle a case of a certain Jew who was accused of spying. This unfortunate man refused to confess to anything [and] maybe he was not even guilty of anything because I had previously had a case of a Jew named Mordka Zikora with an order to review his case within 24 hours and to sentence him as a spy. This man even denied the name that was attributed to him in the indictment and to prove, he referred to the documents found on him during his arrest. These documents [however] were not delivered to me from the Main Staff, while all charges were directed against Mordka and no one else, so I suspended the meeting to go to Kalisz and get documents referred to by the defendant, or to obtain any other evidence that would establish, without any doubt, his real name. I was not thanked for this delay in the court proceedings but because no one could give me this Jew's papers, I was allowed to postpone the trial for a day. In the meantime, my auditor (secretary) gathered information in prisons and found out that our authorities have mistakenly released the real Mordka Zikora and instead sent me another Jew.

26 March [7 April]. Tuesday.

During the night we received an order to depart and marched out at 9 o'clock in the morning. Our regiment's gathering place was set at Skalmierzyce. The main headquarters moved to Rajkovo, and our battalion to Radlow. It is rather incredible to be able to move the theater of military operations from Moscow to the Elbe River in just five months.

It is said that when [Marshal Louis Nicholas] Davout, during his retreat, arrived in Dresden, the city residents sent a deputation to him with a request to spare their main bridge since the Russians had already crossed the Elbe in another place, and that by destroying the bridge, he would only cause them unnecessary harm. With this request, the marshal was offered a precious gift, which he took and then ordered the destruction of one or two arches of the famous bridge, the object of the poor Saxons' anguish.

27 March [8 April]. Thursday.

We departed at 6:30 am. Entered Silesia at Sulmerice and occupied quarters at Honkwitz.

28 March [9 April]. Friday.

A day of rest. I spent the entire day walking in the countryside and observing a vast difference in the lifestyle of Germans and Poles. All the advantages are on the German side.

29 March [10 April]. Saturday.

We departed at 5 am, and by 12 pm, already settled into lodgings at Pardowo. The weather was very warm.

30 March [11 April]. Sunday.

At 2 am I marched with my two companies, the 8th and the 9th, to join the rest of the battalion and follow it. During today's hike, we walked along the borders of the Duchy of Warsaw, which we invaded twice (first time at the village of Ostowo, and the second time at the village of Polus) in order to reach Golesz and continue our journey through Silesia to Trachenberg, where a part of our battalion stopped to assume the duty of guarding the Emperor, while the rest of the battalion went to Żmigród, a village about 1/4 *versta* from the city. The Emperor took an apartment in the Żmigród Castle, and in the evening I had the opportunity to visit Count Arakcheyev, who handed me a letter from Madame B.

31 March [12 April]. Monday.

The Imperial quarters remained in Trachenberg for a day while our battalion departed at 7 am. It marched across the Wincit [?] at Gros Kreylau, where we took up our quarters.

APRIL

1 [13] April. Tuesday.

A day of rest at Gros Kreylau.

2 [14] April. Wednesday.

We crossed the Oder River at Steinau. The King of Prussia was present at the crossing, and we held a parade. The crowds ran toward us, expressing their great joy. The city gate was adorned with inscription in German: "Welcome the Saviors of the Oppressed." After passing Steinau, we made a halt and had enough time to get a breakfast in a tavern which is very important during the campaign. After marching for some distance, I took lodging inside a landowner's house at Herzogwalde where I was perfectly placed.

3 [15] April. Thursday.

We departed at 5 o'clock in the morning. The Imperial quarters moved to Luben, our regimental headquarters to Hainau, while I went to Bruksdorf. During this march we could see the Glatz mountain range that separates Silesia from Bohemia on our left. This area is very picturesque.

4 [16] April. Friday.

The corps headquarters moved to Bunzlau [Bolesławiec], while I was billeted in Gnadenberg. During this march we have come closer to the Bohemian mountains.

5 [17] April. Saturday.

A day of rest at Gnadenberg. This place is inhabited by Moravian brothers or Herrnhuters.[40] It is properly laid out, has a fairly large area with a church in the middle. The Church is surrounded by a small garden, which is very carefully maintained. The cemetery, located near the city, serves also as a place for walking. The monuments are erected symmetrically in the form of a parallelogram, surrounded by trees and

---

[40] Moravian brothers refers to the Moravian Church which came into existence as a result of one of the earliest church reform movements in Bohemia and Moravia in the 15th century.

separated from one another with neat tracks. In one of the parallelograms I counted 22 monuments in width and 23 in length, which is 506, and there were six such parallelograms, meaning there were at least 3036 monuments and, obviously, the number of the dead buried under them would be the same. One hopes that if the residents of Gnadenberg will continue to bury their monks in the same manner, this would become the largest place for walking in the world. The Herrnhuters sect is widespread in this region and their center, Herrnhut, near Gnadenberg. They provide remarkable support for each other. They say that when their Moscow union, known as the Saratov community, let them know that the [Great] Fire had destroyed their property and ruined them, all brothers pitched in to assist the victims so they can resume their trade in the same way as if nothing ever happened to them. The Herrnhuters practice Lutheran religion but with even fewer rituals than other sects of this religion, and with even more simplified rituals compared to other Christian religions. Gnadenberg is inhabited exclusively by artisan and their hand-made knick-knacks are sold here. There is also an orphanage for 25 girls. Manners there are very strict. Some two *versta*s from Gnadenberg one can see Kreuzberg, with a castle built on top of it.

6 [18] April. Sunday.

Due to the battalion commander' illness, I assumed his duties. Today we went through Bunzlau and Naumburg to Schreisbersdorf in Lusatia.[41] The weather was peculiarly northern: it was cold, and raining with hail.

In Bunzlau, there is a clock mechanism that depicts the suffering of Jesus Christ (The Passion) with small figurines that are only 10 vershki tall.

In Naumburg we left Silesia and entered Saxony, or to be precise, Lusatia, which is part of Saxony.

7 [19] April. Monday.

We departed at 5 o'clock in the morning. It was very cold, even snowing, just like in Russia. The Saxons, on surface, welcomed us just as the Prussians did but nevertheless we had been ordered take the same precautions here as in Poland. We camped at Hertz, where a magnificent triumphal arch was erected in our honor. The Saxon coat of arms was replaced by a double-headed Russian eagle. Having passed through

---

[41] A historical region between the Bóbr and Kwisa rivers and the Elbe river in the eastern German states of Saxony and Brandenburg and south-western Poland.

Görlitz, we took up quarters in the village of Zodel. On this march we came very close to the mountains.

8 [20] April. Tuesday.

The entire regiment was supposed to depart at the same time and, for this purpose, we had to concentrate at Reichenbach first. But because the 2nd Battalion was late, we departed by battalions. I personally stopped for breakfast in Reichenbach and then, having lost the way, arrived at Lobau, where I noticed my mistake, asked around for directions and finally found my unit at Sornsig. During this march we have suffered greatly from the cold because the road from Zodel to Reichenbach runs up in the hills. Nikolai came to see me and stayed for the night.

9 [21] April. Wednesday.

A day of rest at Sornsig. We were amazed to hear our native Russian language in the very heart of Germany. These turned out to be settlers who did not want to learn German as enemies of enlightenment.

10 [22] April. Thursday.

The regiment gathered at Hochkirch located 1-2 [Russian] miles [4.5-9 miles] from Sornsig. I brought there the battalion that I [temporarily] commanded and while waiting for the arrival of the remaining two battalions, I occupied myself with studying the battlefield of Frederick the Great. In 1758, this king was at Hochkirch by the Austrian troops under the command of [Marshal Leopold Josef Graf] Daun. The positions occupied by the Prussians were so bad that the King had declared, "If Daun does not attack me here, he should be hanged, but it seems to me that he fears my guns more than the gallows." But unfortunately, this time Daun was not afraid of Friedrich's guns and taking advantage of a fog, he attacked the Prussians. Since that moment the battle had lost for the Prussians. They were fighting not for victory but for the sake of their own salvation. The discipline of the Prussian army was such that, even being caught in the most disadvantaged position, it braced for battle at once and began to retreat under the cover of a single battalion that was left in the village of Hochkirch. With heroic courage, this battalion withstood repeated attacks of the entire Austrian army for the next 12 hours. It perished in its entirety but its unparalleled devotion to duty enabled the rest of the Prussian army to retreat in good order. I saw the church in Hochkirch, where holes made by bullets and cannonball are still visible and attest to the murderous fire to which the Prussian battalion was subjected. Prussian Marshal Keith,[42] who was wounded at the very beginning of the battle, died the same day inside the church; there is still a bench stained with his blood. The Prussian military reveres this bench as a sacred relic and from time to time Prussians appear to take a piece of wood from the bench that is so sacred for them. An urn, placed in the sacristy, designates the place where the remains of the marshal were buried. After inspecting the interior of the church, I climbed up into the bell tower from which you can see the entire battlefield. I would have stayed there for a long time if not for a drum beat that alerted me to the fact that the regiment had already gathered and was ready to depart. So I hastened to lead the battalion.

From Hochkirch, we went to Bautzen, or Budisin, a city founded by the Vandals, judging by the name. We made a halt there, but not long enough to see the nearby castle where Saxon electors once lived. After another [Russian] mile and a half [7 miles], we settled in apartments in Schmölln.

11 [23] April. Friday.

We departed at 5 o'clock in the morning. The regiment gathered at Bischofswerda, then headed along the Dresden road and stopped about one Russian mile [4.6 miles] from the city, taking quarters at Schullwitz.

12 [24] April. Saturday.

At Dresden. Our corps gathered to the gates of Dresden by noon, but the Emperor arrived only by 2 pm.

The Grenaderskii and Pavlovskii Regiments were assigned to the Guard so our [Guard] infantry is now organized into 2 divisions: the first division includes the Preobrazhenskii, Semeyonovskii, Izmailovskii and Jager regiments; the second division comprises of the Litovskii, Grenadier, Pavlovskii and Finlyandskii regiments. In addition, the Prussian Guard has joined us and is deployed in battle order in between our two divisions.

The entire population of Dresden came out to see us, shouting "Hurrah" which they learned after the Glory of Russia. The Emperor and King of Prussia passed in front of the columns deployed on the Altmarkt,[43] where the troops paraded before them.

---

[42] Commanding the rearguard of Frederick's forces was Generalfeldmarschall Jacob von Keith, born James Keith, a Scot from Peterhead.

[43] Old Market Square in Dresden.

We walked in the following order:

1) First Infantry Division of the Imperial Guard.

2) The infantry of the Prussian Guard.

3) Second Infantry Division of the Imperial Guard.

4) 3rd Army Corps, comprising of grenadiers and the Guard Cavalry, both Russian and Prussian, and artillery.

One cannot imagine how surprised were Germans upon seeing a radiant bearing of our troops, because according to the news spread by the French, the Russian army perished the same way as did the French.

I personally was struck by our cavalry which I have not seen since 1812. Then it was in a terrible condition, but today - in a magnificent form.

Young girls, all in white, stood on the sides of the streets and covered our path with flowers; the people called us the deliverers of Europe and expressed a genuine and heartfelt joy. For us it truly was a great and delightful celebration. We were billeted inside Dresden itself. An illumination was held in the evening and the city folk kept filing up the streets.

I used the remainder of the day to see the cathedral, where relics of St. Constance and St. Candelibus. I did not have the opportunity to view the art gallery because it was still closed and, besides, as a measure of precaution, anything that was valuable and magnificent was already moved to Königstein.

13 [25] April. Sunday. The Easter.

The incessant Easter kissing [*khristovanie*][44] by the Russians astonished Saxons, who are not familiar with this custom. After the parade, I spent time walking around the city. The famous bridge over the Elbe has 15 arches, two of which were damaged by Marshal Davout during his retreat. I took a long walk in the Bril gardens overlooking the Elbe and, admiring this marvelous view, I went to a Catholic church, where I listened to a wonderful music. In the evening Italian artists performed opera "La Vestale;" this spectacle was attended by both monarchs, who were enthusiastically greeted. The opera was, in fact, very good.

14 [26] April. Monday.

---

[44] On the Easter, Russians greeted each other with three kisses on the cheeks.

I attended a funeral mass, held in a Catholic church, in memory of the mother of the reigning [Saxon] king, who died 30 years ago.[45] Such service is held every Monday ever since her death. The church was draped in black, the court ladies, still remaining in Dresden, attended dressed in mourning. Once again I had a chance to hear some wonderful music.

After dinner I went to see the art gallery, which was open this time but was nearly empty. It did feature [a painting] of the Moscow Fire.

15 [27] April. Tuesday.

Baron Epschelwitz [?], whom I recently met, invited me to take a walk with him in the evening in Neustadt; it is the part of the city of Dresden that is located on the right bank of the Elbe. It features a very beautiful boulevard and a picturesque square with has an equestrian statue of King of Poland and Elector of Saxony Augustus II in the middle of it. There is also the royal garden with the castle where the King had never lived.

Baron Epschelwitz, his two daughters and I walked for very long time in the garden that was enclosed with a bulwark from which we enjoyed a splendid view.

16 [28] April. Wednesday.

Our regiment was ordered to depart at 7 am but I was allowed to stay in Dresden for a few more hours and departed with Khrapovitskii on horseback only at 2 o'clock in the afternoon. We travelled in rain that kept soaking us wet. We passed through Wilsdruff and Nossen and caught up with our regiment as it rested near Marbach.

17 [29] April. Thursday.

The enemy was quite close to us so we were initially ordered to bivouac, but then this order was canceled, and we were allowed to take up quarters that we occupied together with the Main Headquarters at Geringswalde, after passing through Waldheim.

18 [30] April 18. Friday.

---

[45] Maria Antonia Walpurgis Symphorosa of Bavaria, the wife of Frederick Christian, Elector of Saxony, and mother of King Frederick August III of Saxony, died on 23 April 1780.

We marched through Rochlitz and Geithain to Eschefeld, where we were ordered to take up quarters. In the evening, regimental quartermasters were called up to determine the assignment of spots for our bivouacs at Eschefeld. Our regiment had to depart at once. The night was pitch-black and it rained ceaselessly; naturally, there was nothing tempting about bivouacs in such circumstances and the entire perspective [of spending the night in the open] could hardly please us. Fortunately, a new order soon followed that allowed us to stay at our quarters until 4 am.

19-20 April [1-2 May]. Saturday and Sunday.

We left our quarters at Eschefeld at 5 am on Saturday and, following the orders received the day before, we deployed near this village. We stood there until 1 pm before marching to Lobstadt where we again bivouacked. It was here that for the first time since the Moscow campaign that we heard the sound of gun fire.[46] During the night from Saturday to Sunday a drumbeat woke us up at around 1 am and the entire army, both the Russian and Prussian troops, departed at once.

The joint Command of the Russian and Prussian armies was granted to General of Cavalry Count Wittgenstein because Field Marshal Prince Kutuzov fell ill and stayed behind the army.[47] The movement of our corps had been hampered by the Prussian columns, so that it reached the bivouacs only at 10 am on Sunday. At 3 pm the corps marched out again, this time towards Lutzen where the battle raged since early morning.

Arriving on the battlefield, our corps, kept in reserves, took position behind the center of the Russo-Prussian army. We had to form a rather long line. At this time we occupied the villages: the Gross- and Klein-Gorschen and Rahna. The victory seemed imminent; the Emperor, King of Prussia and Count Wittgenstein came to congratulate us. But as soon as passed in front of our columns, the enemy cannonballs began to reach us. It became clear that despite our gains, the French batteries[48] had, in fact, moved forward and closer to us.

We were ordered to form in battalion columns and march forward. We soon encountered a large number of fleeing Prussian troops that run by us without stopping. We halted not far from the village where we became exposed to a terrible fire of the enemy batteries. It was obvious

---

[46] The gunfire was part of Napoleon's attack on Lutzen and Rippach.

[47] In fact, Kutuzov passed away on 28 April but the army was not yet informed.

[48] Pushin probably refers to two batteries moved forward by General Southam of the 3rd Corps.

that the French had resumed their attacks and captured all of the villages from which we had dislodged them earlier.

This occurred around 6 pm. Our corps maintained its position till late night. It could have easily recaptured the village, located in front of it, but we received no order and therefore limited our actions to simply observing the enemy. At this time, an incident made us laugh. The enemy fire subsided as the darkness descended but suddenly three Prussian light horse artillery guns, under a very brave officer, rushed to us seemingly out of nowhere. These guns took up positions and the [Prussian] officer, upon learning that our brigade commander was Baron Rosen, approached him, put his hand to his cap and said, "Mit eriauben" (with your permission). And then, without waiting for an answer, he ordered, "Erste canon-feer" (first cannon - fire), and the three howitzers began to fire with a remarkable speed. The French, who felt challenged by such an act, responded with some thirty guns, which caused all of us to tell the Prussian artilleryman to go to hell together with his cannon that could not inflict as much damage to the enemy as it did to us. To avoid unnecessary losses, Baron Rosen ordered us to fall back; a detachment of the Prussian cavalry, which stood behind us, was moved forward to cover our withdrawal while the Prussian artillery officer, who was guilty of what had just transpired, shouted, "Ruck vept marche" (march back) and disappeared with their guns just as quickly as he had appeared.

The midnight found us in the midst of another tumult. The Prussian cavalry, which had dismounted to rest, lost a few horses that, to our misfortune, galloped towards us. Because of darkness, we assumed that it was an enemy cavalry charging so we quickly deployed in a square and fired a volley. The cuirassiers, who rushed after their horses, soon explained to us what had just happened but it still took us a long time to restore order that was disrupted by that ill-fated "mit erlauben."

At 10 pm we left the battlefield at Lutzen, proceeded to Pegau, where the Imperial Quarterss also stopped for the night. So we bivouacked there as well. General Miloradovich's corps did not submit reports for that day since it only observed the battle from behind the road to Weissenfels.[49]

21 April [3 May]. Monday.

---

[49] Wittgenstein kept Miloradovich's corps as a reserve, prompting the general to complain, "This is the first time in my life that I hear the sound of gunfire and do not participated in action. If I am not trusted with an army, let me at least have a battalion or a company to fight."

We departed at 5 am. Our corps marched through Lobstadt and Borna and bivouacked at Frohburg.

22 April [4 May]. Tuesday.

Continuing our retreat, we passed through Rochlitz, bivouacking behind the town.

23 April [5 May]. Wednesday

Our corps marched through Waldheim was the corps and bivouacked near the village. Otzdorf. In the evening we could hear a rather intense firefight in the rearguard.[50]

24 April [6 May]. Thursday.

The headquarters of Count Wittgenstein, as well as our corps, was moved, via Nossen, to Wilsdruff.

25 April [7 May]. Friday.

At 3 pm, we underwent a review, and once it was completed, marched towards Dresden. We did not enter this city, where we were so solemnly greeted only a few days ago, but instead marched around it and, after crossing to the right bank of the Elbe, we bivouacked very close to the town.

26 April [8 May]. Saturday.

Marched to Radeberg.

27 April [9 May]. Sunday.

Standing still. Our bivouac had its left flank at Radeberg and right at Augustusbad, famous for its mineral waters. Napoleon entered Dresden.

28 April [10 May]. Monday.

---

[50] There were the rearguard actions at Hartha,

Rumors have it that the French crossed the Elbe. Our corps proceeded to Bischofswerda, where we set up our bivouacs behind the town.

Prince Kutuzov has passed away a few days ago.

29 April [11 May]. Tuesday.

Standing still.

30 April [12 May]. Wednesday.

Our corps marched to Bautzen and after passing through this city, bivouacked at a fortified area.

MAY

1 [13] May. Thursday.

By noon we were ordered to change positions and had to retreat for about 1000 sazhens along the road to Gorlitz. Not a single gunshot could be heard throughout the day.

Today's reports revealed that the king of Saxony [Frederick Augustus] has sided with the French while the Austrian emperor has dispatched his ambassador to the headquarters of Emperor Alexander.

2 [14] May. Friday.

This morning I was busy finishing my correspondence, and then examined our position. On the left flank, the position rested on a wooded hill, then extended to the right, with Bautzen, located in a huge valley, opening in front of it. The right flank was completely exposed but since we had more cavalry than the enemy, the battle field was recognized as advantageous to us, especially since the front of our position was peppered with redoubts and entrenchments. Nevertheless, we were concerned by the vastness of the battlefield, where our army, despite its large size, was seemingly lost in space.

3 [15] May. Saturday.

Finally, after a three-day lull, we heard gun shots. The Imperial Quarters moved from Bautzen to Laubau. The advance guard, under command of General Miloradovich, stretched all the way to Bautzen, but the French made no attempt to advance.

4 [16] May. Sunday.

The whole day passed quietly, except for a few cannon shots exchanged in the evening.

5 [17] May. Monday.

In the morning there was a small skirmish in the advance guard. Barclay de Tolly's army, which was committed to the siege of Thorn,[51] joined us today and took positions on our right flank. This is an important reinforcement.

6 [18] May. Tuesday.

[I am] very grateful that the enemy withdrew after the very first shots fired by our guns.

7 [19] May. Wednesday.

I was on duty. When I came, as usual, to deliver my report to General Lavrov, he told me that the French were moving troops on their left flank. This news was confirmed in the afternoon since at 4 o'clock in the afternoon our corps was moved right up to the village of Purschwitz. It was a spot where our extreme right wing was located but now the troops under the command of General Barclay de Tolly have occupied all nearby heights which the enemy forcefully attacked today. General [Friedrich] Kleist with his Prussians also joined the battle slightly to the left of General Barclay. Our corps was located near Purschwitz, behind General Kleist, without engaging in battle that ended with the fall of darkness.

8 [20] May. Thursday.

The French again attacked Barclay de Tolly. By 4 o'clock in the afternoon, this fighting took a serious turn, and a general battle ensued.

---

[51] The siege of Thorn last from January to 18 April 1813. Barclay de Tolly brought about 12,000 men to the main army.

Our corps was placed under arms. Our advance guard, in the meantime, marched out of Bautzen, which was occupied by the enemy, who then dispatched his skirmishers to the wooded hills on our left flank. Apparently, the enemy's success in this direction prompted the order for our corps to leave its positions at Purschwitz and move to the extreme left wing, where it took up new positions at the bottom of the heights. The Pavlovskii Regiment, deployed inside the woods, forced the enemy skirmishers to fall back. Still, they stopped firing only late in the evening.

Our corps remained at these positions until 10 pm when it rushed forward to take its place in front line, having its left wing on the heights that were still occupied by our skirmishers.

The 3rd Corps took a position behind us, in the second line.

The Emperor came to see us and greeted our soldiers, urging them to fight valiantly tomorrow.

And of course, we were not allowed to take off our uniforms for the night.

9-10 [21-22] May. Friday-Saturday.

The Battle of Bautzen. At daybreak, we were already under arms. There were some 200 guns deployed inside the redoubts in front of us. They began to fire at 6 am. Our battalions were quickly deployed [in line]. In the morning, the French sent all their forces against our right flank and bombarded the rest of our line with their artillery. Batteries located in front of us boldly returned fire.

As the battle began, the 3rd Corps moved forward to support us but then stayed in the front line while we were moved to the second line. At 6 pm, when the enemy gained an upper hand on our right flank, we received the order to retreat. The [Life Guard] Finlyandskii Regiment was dispatched to a small village located to the right from us, in the center of the main position. The rest of the corps, still exchanging fire with the enemy artillery, began retreating by battalions deployed in a remarkable chess formation. The Emperor was delighted by the precision of our maneuver and informed us of his pleasure through his adjutant.

As we came out of range of the French guns, we deployed in marching columns and kept marching throughout the night. By 10 o'clock in the morning, we halted for a few hours after passing Reichenbach, and then resumed our movement at 1 pm, marching beyond Gorlitz, where we took up positions before the end of the day.

11 [23] May. Sunday.

Our corps departed before 6 am. It take a direction to Silesia via Laubau, and bivouacked at Timmendorf.

My cheek became swollen again and I could not stay inside the tent. So I took an apartment in Timmendorf. I cannot fully describe how upset the inhabitants of Silesia are at the prospects of an approaching enemy.

12 [24] May. Monday.

We retreated to Lowenberg. A cannonade was heard in the rearguard.

13 [25] May. Tuesday.

Our corps stopped at Goldberg [Złotoryja]. A cannonade could be again heard today. Zhadovskii, an officer of our regiment, arrived yesterday straight from St. Petersburg but was very poorly received by the officers. Yet, I personally was glad to see him because he told me a lot about my sisters and Madame B.

My cheek is still swollen, so not wanting to risk any complications by remaining in a tent, I again took an apartment at a nearby village.

14 [26] May. Wednesday.

Standing still. My periostitis[52] has not subsided yet so I intended to stay in the village for another day but the intensifying cannonade announced the approach of the enemy and forced me to leave the apartment and return to the camp for the night.

15 [27] May. Thursday.

We were ordered to depart at 3 o'clock at night. Moving off the main road that ran from Goldberg and Liegnitz, our corps turned right and headed into the mountains, where it bivouacked at the village of Zeichau where we remained in anticipation of new orders until 7 pm. At this time the Emperor came to see us. He looked very content and told us that the Austrians have joined us. We then marched in the direction of Jawor and bivouacked about half a [Russian] mile [2.3 miles] from Hennersdorf.

The rearguard was again involved in an action. Our corps and the 3rd Corps were instructed to support it if it became necessary but, despite a

---

[52] See note 39.

strong cannonade that gradually came closer to us, our succor proved to be unnecessary.

16 [28] May. Friday.

We slept peacefully until 5 am when departed through Jawor and camped out behind Strigau. The enemy made almost no movements today and only a slight cannonade was heard throughout the day.

17 [29] May. Saturday.

Not moving. Everything was quiet today and there were no actions. The enemy captured ten of our guns on the road to Breslau.[53]

18 [30] May. Sunday.

Standing still.

19 [31] May. Monday.

Our corps headed for Schweidnitz and encamped at a fortified position outside the town.

20-21 May [1-2 June]. Tuesday-Wednesday.

Not moving. We spent the day reinforcing our position and repairing fortifications at Schweidnitz.

22 May [3 June]. Thursday.

Despite all the efforts expended on repairing fortifications at Schweidnitz, we departed from our camp at 2 am on Thursday night and marched in the direction of Strehlen via the village of Gross-Wilnau that was located close to Nimptsch [Niemcza] where we set up our camp. We suffered greatly from the heat and dust.

23 May [4 June]. Friday.

---

[53] Pushin refers to General Sebastiani's raid near Sprottau that led to the capture of either 22 cannon and 500 prisoners (French sources) or 13 cannon and 200 prisoners (Russian sources)

The Main Headquarters departed during the night while we woke up expecting to follow it at once. However, the order to march came rather later and the division departed only at 5 pm. It proceeded to Strelen, where we set up a camp, with our left wing anchored on the town.

Anticipating that this march would be resume at night and not having a battalion to command, I traveled ahead with Prince [Sub Lieutenant of the Life Guard Semeyonovskii Regiment Ivan] Sherbatov. Despite a good progress made by our horses, we reached Strelen only by the end of the day and, taking advantage of the town's proximity from our camp, we found comfortable lodgings there.

24 May [5 June]. Saturday.

Standing still. We were informed that the Emperor would be in Strelen soon but he has not arrived yet.

Our reserves joined us today so our corps considerably increased in size.

I was busy visiting my acquaintances. I saw Fuchs and [Colonel Dmitri] Lyapunov, my old commander.

25 May [6 June]. Sunday.

For some time now we have heard about the cessation of hostilities [at the Armistice of Pleischwitz. Today, this rumour was finally confirmed even though the daily order made no mention of it.

Our corps departed before 10 am. My regiment made a very long march, proceeding through Reichenbach [Dzierżoniów] to Langen-Bielau, where it took up quarters.

The Imperial Quarters moved to Peterswaldau while the headquarters of our army commander Barclay de Tolly is at Reichenbach.

The city of Breslau, located between two lines of demarcation, has been declared as neutral. By this order, our army's rear touched Bohemia.

26 May [7 June]. Monday.

I visited Reichenbach, which is located slightly more than one [Russian] mile [~5 miles] away from Langen-Bielau.

27 May [8 June]. Tuesday.

Today was our regimental review so I traveled to Reichenbach to attend it. Some Austrian general was present at the review, and the Emperor kept talking to him.

I found Count Arakcheyev digging in a small garden adjacent to his apartment. He worked there as if it were his property.

29 May [10 June]. Thursday.

Our battalion assumed the guard duty at the Emperor's quarters and since I commanded the guar outposts, I spent the entire day at Reichenbach. I walked for a long time inside the castle garden which is superbly maintained. Germans, it seems, love gardening, and every farmer has a small garden. Count Arakcheyev acts like as German. I found him again digging in the garden of his host, and I never suspected he loves farming so much. So overall I had a rather lovely day, although I cannot say the same about the night. Unable to find any room to sleep, I had to go into *hauptwache* [military prison] where instead of a bed I only got a little bit of straw, just like on bivouac.

30 May [11 June]. Friday.

After the changing of the guard, I went to Langen-Bielau. The village is stretched from one end to the other for at least three *versta*s [~2 miles] so when we wanted to visit each other, we had to take trips that were longer that to Reichenbach or Peterswaldau. Fortunately, our General Potemkin established his quarters right in the center of the village. I stopped by his apartments today on my return from Peterswaldau.

I settled down with Khrapovitskii on the second floor while the ground floor was occupied by the owner of the house. He treated us to a simply but very good lunch and his two daughters – the beautiful Julia and the little Teresa, who is also quite pretty – waited our table. As usual Khrapovitsky flirted with the former while I dallied with the latter, but we occasionally confused them, especially when one of us was not at home, and mistook Theresa for Julia and Julia for Teresa.

31 May [12 June]. Saturday.

The weather is lovely and the wooded hills surrounding Langen-Bielau present a picturesque view, especially when their mountain tops are shrouded in clouds.

JUNE

1 [13] June. Sunday.

Today is the Trinity Holiday, which is the holiday of the Izmailovskii Regiment which attended at the mass in Peterswaldau. After the mass, the soldiers enjoyed breakfast in the garden. The Emperor [Alexander] and King of Prussia [Frederick William] and his young princes attended the luncheon. Then the regiment passed in a ceremonial march in front of the monarchs, and officers of the regiment dined with the Emperor.

3 [15] June. Tuesday.

In the evening I visited Reichenbach, hoping to see [Ensign Ivan] Burtsov [of the 4th Corps' Quartermaster Service], but he had already departed.

8 [20] June. Sunday.

For the past three or four days, the Emperor has been gone. His Majesty went to Bohemia - some say he was going to confer with the Austrian emperor, others argued that he attended a review of Austrian troops, who were expected to join us for a joint action against the French.

General Potemkin decided to arrange a carousel in Langen-Bielau. I saw it for the first time today since it has been raining until now.

11 [23] June. Wednesday.

I dined at General Potemkin's apartment, where it was positively asserted that the Emperor had not yet seen the Austrian emperor, who was expected in Dresden.

12 [24] June. Thursday.

The Emperor has returned to Peterswaldau.

13 [25] June. Friday.

Wanting to learn the news, I went to see General Potemkin, who visited Peterswaldau after the Emperor's return but the mystery [surrounding the Emperor's trip] is impenetrable, and all that I could learn from the general was that His Majesty had told him that he had seen Austrian troops.

The Imperial Suite assures everyone that the Emperor had not seen the Austrian emperor, but he had many meetings with the first minister of the Austrian [Klemens von Metternich] and that one of these Meetings even lasted continuously for nine hours. Some people say that there will be a major review on the 18th and it will be attended by several Austrian generals.

14 [26] June. Saturday.

French bulletins continued to advertise the devotion of the Saxon king [to Napoleon]. It might be true when it comes to the king himself, but the population feels quite differently. I learned today about an incident that confirms this. An officer of the Guard artillery, named Timan, was captured at the battle of Bautzen and sent to Dresden. Upon seeing him, one of the city residents secretly approached him and told him quietly, "I have only two ecus (small currency) but nevertheless I would like, as all my fellow citizens do, to help out Russian prisoners, who, as usual, lack any means of supporting themselves. So please do not offend me by your refusal and take half of my treasure, which is just one *ecu.* " Timon was very touched by this expression of friendliness and he assured us that such incidents occurred many times during his captivity. In fact, his release was the result of the Saxons, who are loyal to the Russians. The prisoners were moved from Dresden to Leipzig. One of the city residents offered Timan and his two friends, Prussian officers, his help in escaping their captivity. He brought them clothes and passports of the Leipzig students. He then gave them a guide who led them to Teplitz, from where they could easily find their way to the main headquarters of the Russo-Prussian army. As they journeyed from Leipzig to Teplitz though the areas occupied by the French, the local [Saxons] posed them as students and placed them under protection of village elders, who were aware of this secret and yet never thought of betraying them. Such attitudes among the Saxons clearly did not confirm official proclamations of their allegiance to the French.

15 [27] June. Sunday.

I visited Peterswaldau to see Count Arakcheyev, who told me that he plans to travel to Warsaw on the 19th. He gave me letters from St. Petersburg. I was aggrieved by this news since the count's departure meant an end to the delivery of my correspondence.

16 [28] June. Monday.

At 6 pm, we launched training exercises. All residents of Langen-Bielau poured out to watch them.

18 [30] June. Wednesday.

The Grand Review. Our troops lined up in two lines in a vast plain between Peterswaldau and Langen-Bielau. Only infantry was deployed: two infantry divisions of the Russian Imperial Guard and four battalions of the Prussian Royal Guard. King of Prussia and the Princes arrived by 10 am. They were followed, at a short distance, by the princesses of the Royal House of Prussia[54] with all the great ladies of the court in sumptuous carriages.

After following the Emperor along the both lines [of troops], the two carriages stopped next to the monarchs, and troops moved at a brisk pace in front of them. During the review, I commanded the 1st battalion of our [Life Guard Semeyonovskii] regiment.

19 June [1 July]. Monday.

The 1st Battalion conducted training exercises in the presence of the Emperor and then took over the guard duty. For 24 hours, I commanded the guard outposts in Peterswaldau. After the parade I went to see Count Arakcheyev, but did not catch him since he had departed at 5:00 am.

The King of Prussia with his family dined with the Emperor, who was extremely gracious. He accompanied the princesses to their carriages. After their departure, the Emperor held up musicians from our regiment and began studying with them the notes of the Austrian marching music, which he brought back from his trip to Bohemia. The purpose of the trip was clearly political but yet, this man has a very strange character: the

---

[54] The author later added the following comment: "Among them was the future Russian Empress Alexandra Feodorovna, then still Princess Charlotte." Princess Frederica Louise Charlotte Wilhelmina of Prussia was the eldest surviving daughter and fourth child of Frederick William III, King of Prussia, and Louise of Mecklenburg-Strelitz, and a sister of future King Frederick William IV of Prussia and of Wilhelm I, German Emperor. She married Grand Duke Nicholas, the future emperor of Russia, in July 1817.

most pressing and serious affairs could not distract him from his passion to get involved in the most trifling things.

20 June [2 July]. Friday.

As he prepared to leave for the parade, the Emperor gave orders to stop drum beats and very graciously talked to a few soldiers and me. He was in very good spirits.

After the changing of the guard, I returned to Langen-Bielau. New general and our old comrade Baron [Ivan] Diebitch came to see us. Rapid promotion and success have not changed him and he treated us as cordially and hospitably as though he was still a junior officer serving with us. Diebitch, the son of a senior aide to Frederick the Great, was invited to Russia by Emperor Paul and was enlisted as an ensign in the Life Guard Semeyonovskii Regiment during the early years of Emperor Alexander's reign. He was already a lieutenant when I joined the regiment. General [Leontii] Depreradovich[55] did not want to assign him to a guard duty on the Kamennyi Island[56] because Diebitch was quite ugly. So Diebitch beseeched me as the battalion adjutant to help him in this matter and I took him to General Depreradovich; one may say that Diebitch forced the general to revise his decision. During the battle at Guttstadt [in 1807, he advised the Grand Duke [Constantine Pavlovich] in selecting positions for artillery batteries. His counsel was accepted and produced such good results that Diebitch was awarded the Order of St. George (4th class). In 1806[57] he joined His Imperial Majesty's Suite, as the main headquarters was then called, and received the rank of a lieutenant colonel of the quarter master service. He served with a remarkable zeal at the headquarters of Count Wittgenstein in 1812.

21 June [3 July]. Saturday.

Khrapovitsky and I had an early lunch so we could visit Frankenstein, a small town on the road between Nimptsch and Wartha. The road from Langen-Bielau to Frankenstein ran through the mountains. On our right

---

[55] Depreradovich commanded the LG Semeyonovskii regiment in 1799-1807.

[56] Kamennyi Island was one of the islands in the Neva delta where Saint Petersburg was located. By the early 19th century, the island was the residence of the cream of crop of the Russian society, where the Russian grandees had their summer retreats. At the eastern-most tip of the island there was the Kamennoostrovsky Palace where Emperor Alexander resided.

[57] Pushin is mistaken since Diebitch was appointed to the Suite in 1810.

110

we could see the fortress of Silberberg [Srebrna Góra] built on three very steep hills.

Frankenstein is as large as Schweidnitz. However, German cities are all very similar. They usually have a large central square that is intersected by the main street while other streets join at other corners of the square. The city hall and the church are erected in the middle of the town and the rest of the city is divided by cross-streets, whose number depends on the size of the town. Houses are usually two and three-story tall but so narrow that they seldom have more than three or four windows on the facade. This description does not apply to Dresden, Bautzen, Gorlitz and other large cities but is very appropriate to town like Frankenstein. As soon as you enter a small German town, you are immediately surrounded by a crowd of half-naked boys who offer their services to you: they take your horses, perform any of your instructions, lead you to a tavern and kiss your hands whenever you give them a few coins. We experienced it all in Frankenstein where we settled at the inn "Black Eagle". Our stay here proved to be brief. This journey was occasioned by our curiosity as well as the utmost need to buy boots that this area is famous for. Having accomplished all that we came here for, we immediately embarked on a return trip to Langen-Bielau, arriving there by 8 pm.

22 June [4 July]. Sunday.

The Emperor ordered to gather all the children of the regimental priests in Peterswaldau where they sang in a church choir. After the mass he ordered to give a silver ruble to each child but his generosity displeased the head of the Imperial Quarters who stated publicly that the Emperor would soon be left without a penny.

My brother Nicholas was also in Peterswaldau and took him with me to dine at Langen-Bielau. In the evening, we attended a rather comical concert.

23 June [5 July]. Monday.

I spent the day with my cousins, who are quartered in Schlaupitz, which is about two [Russian] miles away from Reichenbach. On my way back, I got completely soaked in a heavy rain.

25 June [7 July]. Wednesday.

We travelled in a large company to Gnadenfrei [Pilawa Gorna], the colony of Herrnhuters,[58] a few miles from Langen-Bielau and

111

Reichenbach. Upon arriving there, our immediate concern was to take care of our horses and to order a lunch at a local tavern. While our food was cooked, we had enough time to explore the town, and here are my observations. Gnadenfrei is quite similar to Gnadenberg, which I have already described in my notes on April 4-5 of this year. Its population is almost entirely engaged in manufacturing. There are all kinds of textiles and cloths available here. The church is unadorned and does not even feature a crucifixion. The choirs and organ – that is the extent of its adornment. There are two schools, one for boys and one for girls: they are very good and very meticulously maintained. The French language is taught there; youngsters also learn different skills and crafts that are appropriate to their age, and their creations are then sold for the benefit of schools.

26 June [8 July]. Thursday.

I dined with [the officers] of the [Life Guard] Lithuanian Regiment which is deployed at Scheifersdorf, about one [Russian] mile north of Reichenbach.

27 June [9 July]. Friday.

Many of our officers went to Frankenstein: the younger [Peter] Chaadayev and I traveled in a chaise while the rest rode on horses. My companion drew my attention to one thing that escaped me during my first visit to Frankenstein. It is surrounded by a wall with loopholes, one of which is a square shaped, some 12-15 sazhens tall and inclined from its base, so that one side forms a sharp angle while the other - obtuse angle.

After a lunch in Frankenstein, Chaadayev and I went to Peterwitz, a village famous for its mineral waters, located about half a [Russian] mile north-east from Frankenstein. It was already 9 pm when finished bathing in waters. Our driver lost his way, took us through the mountains, and it was already past the midnight when he stopped in the middle of the woods and told us that he was lost and did not know where to go. We sent him to look for a guide and, fortunately, he found a miller and returned with him just quarter an hour later. We took the miller with us, even though he was lightly dressed and the night was cold. He led us to the main road and we returned to Langen-Bielau only at 3 o'clock in the morning.

---

[58] Pushin refers to the members of the Moravian Church, also known as the Bohemian Brethren, an evangelical Protestant denomination that traces its origins from the 15th century, and emphasizes Christian unity, personal piety, and missionary spirit.

29 June [11 July]. Sunday.

I held a lunch [for officers].

30 June [12 July]. Monday.

Bakunin and Khrapovitsky spent two days with me and left only this afternoon. I learned that the Emperor is absent since the 27th [9 July] and it is said that he travelled to meet the Swedish Crown Prince [Bernadotte].

JULY

1 [13] July. Tuesday.

People say that the truce has been extended. It is highly desirable that we quickly depart from Langen-Bielau. Although our men are still healthy, we witness local funerals on daily basis and I am afraid that this pestilence will spread to us as well. These funerals are performed quite solemnly. The procession is preceded by little boys, walking in pairs, carrying crosses and singing hymns. They are followed by a coffin, pastor and a few old men in three-cornered hats and black robes, and, finally, women in black lace, aprons, scarves, gloves and white cap with a big bow on their forehead and big baskets in their hands. These attire belongs to the more prosperous and wealthy residents and are worn not only during the days of mourning, but also for all important occasions, for example, the mass and other holidays. This clothing is passed from generation to generation as a dowry for the wealthier brides. Otherwise, [local] Germans mainly walk barefoot and only few young men and old people wear shoes throughout the week, while the rest of the population uses them only on Sundays. Young men put on their coats only on holidays, and their daily attire usually includes a cloth jacket and a round hat. When old women go out dressed in their festive costumes, they always carry a straw hat but I have never seen one of them put it, instead they always hold them in their hands. The poor, comprising the working class [*rabochii klass*], have similar but completely worn out attire and their dirty feet are disgusting. These people work like oxen, almost never eat meat and subsist almost exclusively on potatoes.

2 [14] July. Wednesday.

The Emperor returned yesterday to Peterswaldau. It seems that the armistice will be extended indeed. I learned this news from General Potemkin, who had spent several days in Landeck, a small town in Silesia, about two [Russian] miles south-west of Glatz. He saw the Prussian royal family there and heard this news of Princess Charlotte herself.

3 [15] July. Thursday.

The Emperor departed again, but no one knows where or why.

5 [17] July. Saturday.

In view of the parade that our regiment is scheduled to attend, I was forced to go to Peterswaldau, where I met the newly returned Count Arakcheyev. He told me that the truce will last until the 28th. He also handed me a letter and a very lovely gift from Madame B. I did not know how to thank the count; Madame B. does not cease to care about me.

6 [18] July. Sunday.

While attending the Mass, I learned that the Emperor has returned at 4 o'clock in the morning. The purpose of his visit remains an impenetrable secret; while dining with Svechin and [Ensign Alexander] Simonov [of the Life Guard Preobrazhenskii Regiment], I only heard that His Majesty was very busy these days and often spent whole nights at work.

9 [21] July. Wednesday.

I dined at [Lieutenant General Nikolai] Borozdin's[59] quarters in Reichenbach. There I learned about the French defeat at Vittoria in Spain. The battle took place on June 21- 22 (or July 9-10 under new style calendar). The French lost 150 guns and their entire train.

11 [23] July. Friday.

I travelled with Colonel Nabokov to Frankenstein.

13 [25] July. Sunday.

---

[59] Borozdin commanded a brigade in the 1st Cuirassier Division.

I was on duty in Peterswaldau. All generals attended a dinner with the Emperor, many later talked about the resumption of hostilities. Some claim that Count Langeron's corps and parts of the Prussian army are already preparing for the campaign. Before the dinner, I paid a visit to Count Arakcheyev but he no letters from Madame R, which made me unhappy.

14 [26] July. Monday.

As my duty ended, I went back to Langen-Bielau. The troops, who were moved into a camp, returned back to their quarters.

15 [27] July. Tuesday.

The Emperor attended my regiment's maneuvers. He ordered to remove all restrictions that were imposed [on my estate] because of my father's debts.[60]

After the training exercises, the Emperor and the King ate breakfast together. The Emperor then immediately traveled to see the Grand Duke, where he will spend the night. He will conduct a review of some 80 cavalry squadrons tomorrow.

17 [29] July. Thursday.

The Emperor returned to Peterswaldau.

18 [30] July. Friday.

I went to see Khrapovitsky in Peterwitz. During my first visit there it was already too late in the day and I could not do any sightseeing because of lack of time. This time, I inspected everything, and greatly suffered for it. Baths are incredibly filthy and the tavern is quite disgusting so I was unable to get anything to eat. So we were compelled to travel to Frankenstein, where we dine and remained until 8 pm.

20 July [1 August]. Sunday.

---

[60] Sergei Pushin owed a enormous sum of 17,000 rubles to various debtors and was unable to pay it, which prompted the imperial authorities to impose restrictions on his use of the property in 1808.

Today a general review of the entire Guard infantry was held in the plain between Peterswaldau and Langen-Bielau. After the parade, we attended the Mass held at the [Imperial] court, following which Nikolai and I returned to our quarters for lunch. Our cousin Ivan traveled for a few days to Bialystok, where his regiment's reserve battalion is stationed. Sinyavin told me that the Congress in Prague is already three days underway. He assured me that Napoleon would spare nothing to achieve peace which is essential for him since he currently can deploy only 250,000 men against our army that has increased to some 700,000 men.

22 July [3 August]. Tuesday.

I was invited to dine with [Major General Constantine] Poltoratsky [who commanded the Nasheburgskii Infantry Regiment], but periostitis prevented me from accepting his invitation and I could not go anywhere. I again woke up with a swollen cheek, and spent the entire day completely alone and in terrible anguish. All my roommates were dining out.

23 July [4 August]. Wednesday.

My inflammation slightly subsided so I was able to go out.

25 July [6 August]. Friday.

The Emperor, who has been residing in Landeck since the 20th [1 August] and attending the princesses, reviewed the 3rd Corps at Nimpton today and returned to Peterswaldau.

27 July [8 August]. Sunday.

I went to Peterswaldau today to cultivate my relationship with Count Arakcheyev, but he was so busy that I did not even have time to tell two words to him. Today, a new personality appeared at the court - Prince Platon Zubov, the well-known favorite of the Empress Catherine. He stood among other courtiers and no one paid attention to him. It is clearly a different era. People wondered why he appeared here since he was not a military man.

28 July [9 August]. Monday.

The Congress of Prague has finally ended. The French envoy, the duc de Vicence (Caulaincourt) acted rather arrogantly. He began describing the exploits of the French army, but the allure it once held was demolished after 1812 and he was emphatically told that the envoys had gathered in Prague not to listen to the French bulletins but to negotiate peace. He was offered conditions sine qua non and since they were not accepted, the Austrians have announced that from now on they are our allies, and will embark on campaign the following day.

29 July [10 August]. Tuesday.

Our regiment left Langen-Bielau around noon today. We marched to Silberberg, where we stopped on bivouacs. Our entire corps concentrated here.

30 July [11 August]. Tuesday.

We marched out at 4 am, and after passing by Silberberg, we proceeded to Neyrod. Our camp was set up near this city.

31 July [12 August]. Thursday.

Standing still.

AUGUST

1 [13] August. Friday.

We entered Bohemia, marching through Braunau to Police, where we bivouacked.

2 [14] August. Saturday.

At Bivouacs near Gross-Skalice, Yesterday and today we had very tiring marches. We did not have to cover large distance but had to walk for prolonged periods of time, often for over 10 hours, because of poor roads that we had to take in the mountains. Apparently, the local population is thrilled to see us. Unlike all their neighbors, the Bohemians are the least similar to Germans. In fact, they are more akin to Russians since their origins and language is of Slavic descent.

3 [15] August. Sunday.

Our corps departed at 4 am. It crossed the Elbe at Joromice [Jaromer] about half a [Russian] mile above Jozefstal, a strongly fortified city, and bivouacked at Nedeliste, a village located between Josefstal and Königingrätz.

General [Jean] Moreau has recently arrived from America and he passed by us today. He rode in a carriage dressed in civilian clothing and accompanied by [Russian diplomat Pavel] Svinin whom I knew well in St. Petersburg.

4 [16] August. Monday.

Still standing at Nedeliste. In Bohemia, people are as hospitable as in Russia. Baron de Stepflinger, landowner from the vicinity of Jozefstal, visited our bivouacs the day before and invited us to dine with him if we did not depart today. So we - Polignac, Fensch, Glazenap and I – mounted our horses to take advantage of his invitation. The baron lived in the village of Velhoven, which is about one [Russian] mile away from Nedeliste, and the rain drenched us both as traveled there and returned back. But we were greeted with open arms and treated to a wonderful dinner. The host's daughter, the pretty Lydia Stepflinger, was extremely gracious to us. Many Bohemian customs are similar to ours, for example, they are as fond of hors d'œuvre [*zakuska*] as we are; before you sit down at the table, you served a vodka which the locals call *slivovice* [plum brandy], which we drank to the memory of our common ancestors with great pleasure, especially since we were miserable and soaked to the bone.

5 [17] August. Tuesday.

We marched for fifteen hours straight, and approaching Prague, we halted on bivouacs near Slušavec.

6 [18] August. Wednesday.

Our corps advanced for another 4 [Russian] miles and bivouacked at Laušice. Today is the holiday of the Life Guard Preobrazhenskii Regiment and I was invited to a dinner. I had a chance to see an extraordinary man, who had no arms and did everything with his legs. He could write, cut, shave and comb himself, take tobacco, and perform such skilful card tricks that many will not be able to repeat them with hands.

7 [19] August. Thursday.

Our corps again moved to the left bank of the Elbe, crossing at Elbe-Kostelec, where we set up our bivouacs. We are just two miles from Prague.

8-9 [20-21] August. Friday and Saturday.

Our regiment departed during the night from Thursday to Friday and in two hours crossed the Moldau [Vltava] River. After a stop to prepare food, we marched for the entire day. At 8 pm, we passed through the village of Kmetnovec, continued to march throughout the night and stopped only at 8 am on Saturday morning at Klumšan [?]. While the regiment covered this distance, I, having no battalion to command, travelled differently. I did not eat anything during a halt after the crossing the Moldau, so by the evening I felt very hungry and went ahead [of the troops] with several officers. Along the way, we saw a rather pleasant looking house and stopped by to inquire if we could lunch there. An old woman, who lived there, agreed to a cook for us and made us wait for two hours before feeding us a pitiable soup, which ended up being our entire meal. During that time our corps had marched ahead so we had to trot for some distance in order to catch up with it. The night was very dark and the rain poured down incessantly. Our artillery, moving in the corps' tail, was passing through Kmetnovec precisely when we caught up with the corps. Knowing for certain that the corps would continue marching throughout the night, I decided to stay here overnight. It was only 8 pm but there were no lights inside the houses so we found ourselves in a major quandary concerning accommodation, when by chance we saw one house, taller than others, that was still brightly illuminated. So we decided to go there and knocked on the door. The door immediately opened, and the owner, Pastor Gremowski himself appeared and invited us to stay with him. Of course, we did not let him wait for us and to our great satisfaction, just half an hour after our arrival, the hospitable Pastor Gremovski ordered to prepare a very nice dinner for us. After the dinner, which we consumed with great pleasure, we immediately went to sleep and the Pastor had arranged clean beds for us. We slept until 5 am and were served coffee as soon as we woke up. After thanking Pastor Gremowski for the hospitality he had shown to us, we mounted our horses and caught up with our corps just as it began setting up its bivouacs.

10 [22] August. Sunday.

The corps departed at noon, passed through Lown, a pretty large town, crossed the Eger [Ohre] River and bivouacked at Brix at 8 pm. The closer we get to Saxony, the more the landscape improves and the people seem to be more refined.

11 [23] August. Monday.

In the morning, many officers, believing we would be given a day of rest, prepared to visit Brix but they were soon recalled back to the camp. We then moved through Dux and Teplitz to Sobohleben, where our division bivouacked. The 2nd Guard Division separated from us at Brix and marched to the left in the direction of Georgental. I bid farewell to my brother Nikolai, not knowing where and when we will see each other again.

It was very late in the day when our division marched through Teplitz. I stopped in town to spend the night with Pushkin. We took a furnished apartment and quietly fell asleep.

12 [24] August. Tuesday.

We stayed in Teplitz until 11 am, toured local mineral baths and then joined the division, which spent the entire day at Sobohleben.

13 [25] August. Wednesday.

The division departed at 8 o'clock in the morning. We entered Saxony through Peterswalde [Petrovice] and proceeded to Holenb [?], where we were initially ordered to stop. But this order was soon countermanded and the division marched farther before bivouacking at Cotta.

We could hear the sound of gunfire from the direction of Konigstein. It was the 2nd Corps, whose reserve we comprised, trying to prevent the French crossing of the Elbe.

14 [26] August. Thursday.

At dawn, the fighting broke out at Konigstein. Our division was placed under arms at 6 pm. It rained heavily. The Main Army is engaged in a battle at Dresden.

15 [27] August. Friday.

We were commanded to depart at 3 am on the night from Thursday to Friday. It rained incessantly in a refreshing wind. As our division reached Dohna, it received the order to turn and proceed to Pirna to support Count Osterman, who was already fighting the enemy. The combat was limited to the skirmishers only. In the evening, as it became clear that the enemy was not attacking, we were ordered to pile our arms and rest. The Main Army retreated from Dresden.

16 [28] August. Saturday.

The battle in valleys. At 8 am, the division was under arms. We deployed by battalions in two lines and advanced in this formation towards the ridge, at whose bottom the jagers and the 2nd Corps were already fighting the enemy. The [the Life Guard Semeyonovskii Regiment's] 3rd Battalion [which Pushin commanded] , deployed on the extreme left wing of the second line, moved up to the extreme left wing of the first line. General Count Osterman-Tolstoy took over command of all troops gathered to Pirna. This force included the remains of 3rd Corps and one Guard division; in addition, there were several squadrons of cavalry. When the 3rd Battalion lined up with the rest of the troops of the 1st line, I noticed that our columns stretched beyond the line of skirmishers on the left flank. Therefore, I offered the general to send me with a few skirmishers to extend the skirmisher line. He agreed, giving me two officers and 60 soldiers. As soon as I arranged the skirmisher line, one of our officers, Khrushchev, was wounded, and I was ordered to fall back since our columns were maneuvering with their right flank towards Berggieshubel. A squadron of the Tatar Uhlans covered my retreat. Climbing on a hill, I observed that our division was already far away, and rushed in its wake. At this time, the French under General Vandamme captured Berggieshubel and several other places along the route to Teplitz. So several battalions were dispatched in various directions to drive the French back and enable the division to pass. I rallied the survivors of the 3rd Battalion, which had lost a lot of people after one such expedition. One battalion of the [Life Guard] Preobrazhenskii Regiment attacked Berggieshubel while two battalions of the [Life Guard] Semeyonovskii Regiment charged into Hellendorf. Moving all along, the Division, finally reached Peterswalde by 10 pm and, having no French troops on the road to Teplitz, it took up positions. All battalions that fought separately during the day rejoined the division at this point and the darkness facilitated their retreat.

17 [29] August 17. Sunday.

Battle at Kulm. The French attacked our outposts. At dawn, our division, deployed in battalion columns, retreated from the Kulm heights. It stopped at the entrance into a valley, with its left wing anchored on the wooded heights. Here we received the ordered to hold ground and not to retreat an inch since the Main Army, having failed at Dresden, was hurrying to our aid via Teplitz. This was not, however, an easy order to fulfill. We faced General Vandamme who had 40,000 men while the reinforcements that the Main Army promised us, could not arrive in time because, first, the triumphant enemy was attacking [the Main Army itself] and, secondly, it had to pass through the Erzgebirge Mountains that separate Saxony from Bohemia. The 2nd Corps, which had been fighting for five days straight, already had too few people and our division, consisting of four regiments, suffered heavy losses. Overall, our forces did not exceed 10,000 men.

Despite our difficulties, we immediately proceeded to attack. The first line turned to face the enemy and rushed towards the French as soon as they emerged from a narrow gorge onto the valley of Kulm. Most of General Vandamme's corps was still in the narrow gorge when its advance guard, completely unprepared for the attack, was overwhelmed and routed. At the same time the Guard jagers occupied the woods, located on our left, and, with their usual gallantry, engaged the enemy skirmishers. Initially they gained an upper hand but despite their bravery, they were then forced to fall back because of the enemy's numerical superiority. The [Life Guard Semeyonovskii Regiment's] 3rd Battalion, deployed in the second line, was sent to reinforce them. It entered the woods and drove the French beyond the mill, which they occupied. But as the French skirmishers, seeking to seize the mountain top, tried to turn our left flank, His Majesty's 1st Company marched into the woods and restored the balance so that by 12 o'clock the 3rd Battalion could again come out of the woods and deploy in reserves at the edge of the woods.

In the meantime, the French, having recovered from the initial surprise, moved almost all of their forces out of the gorge into the valley and attacked the center of our position with superior forces. From then on, all of our infantry was engaged in the battle, and only two His Majesty's companies – 1st of the Preobrazhenskii Regiment and 1st of the Semyenovskii Regiments – remained in reserve. The Chevalier Guard and Horse Guard Regiment, which arrived by then, took up positions on the extreme right flank and stood beyond the ravine, the sole protection of this flank

It was a terrible moment.

After a heroic defense, the French numerical superiority prevailed. The jagers retreated along the entire line and the enemy captured villages that comprised our center, and kept advancing everywhere except in the forest, where he made only limited gains. At this time, General Diebitch arrived on the battlefield, bringing several squadrons of the Guard uhlans and dragoons, who charged with exceptional swiftness at enemy columns. The French fled and our infantry charged forward at once. It was the start of the complete breakdown of the enemy army, which fled back to its reserves and no longer dared to attack.

On our left flank, when the enemy recaptured the mill in the woods, I was sent with two companies of the 3rd Battalion to help the jagers in reclaiming the mill. I accomplished it at once, losing only a few officers.

It was already 6 o'clock in the evening. I remained in the woods until 10 pm and the French showed no intentions of attempting anything serious, only firing a few shots from time to time to entertain themselves. Our first reinforcement came with [Major] General [Dmitri] Pyshnitskii,[61] who brought several infantry battalions and the 3rd Corps. They replaced me in the woods. I joined my battalions which had proceeded, with the rest of the division, to Sobohleben.

At dawn on the 18th [30 August], we again heard the sound of gunfire. The 3rd Corps deployed in the first line, and the 1st Guards Division in the second line. By 10 am, the 2nd Guard Division had arrived on the battlefield and I was thrilled to see my brother Nikolai. Hungarian infantry appeared almost at the same time. The 3rd corps attacked the French, who fled by noon. The cavalry pursued them. General Vandamme, 80 guns and numerous prisoners fell into our hands. The victory was complete. We settled in bivouacs on the battlefield.

19 [31] August. Tuesday.

Our corps concentrated earlier today and we marched to Teplitz, where we set up our bivouacs. The Emperor and the Prussian king are also in Teplitz.

20 August [1 September]. Wednesday.

---

[61] Pyshnitskii commanded the 4th Infantry Division.

We served a Te Deum service in celebration of the victory won at Kulm. On this occasion, our entire corps first stood under arms and then moved in a ceremonial march in front of the monarchs.

Our [Life Guard Semeyonovskii] regiment suffered such heavy losses that instead of three battalions, we could deploy only two battalions.[62] Everyone was struck by the dazzling view of our forces – truly, they were dressed as immaculately as they usually are in St. Petersburg. After the parade, our troops again occupied their positions while I paid a visit to Count Arakcheyev, who was also quartered in Teplitz.

21 August [2 September]. Thursday.

A Catholic Mass. Two Austrian divisions moved in a ceremonial march in front of the monarchs.

22 August [3 September]. Friday.

[Today was] the review of artillery.

23 August [4 September]. Saturday.

[Today was] the review of the cavalry, which I also attended. It was impossible not to notice the superiority of the Russian and Prussian troops over the Austrians.

24 August [5 September]. Sunday.

A solemn liturgy for the corps [was held today]. The church was organized inside a tent. The Emperor and King of Prussia were present at the mass.

25 August [6 September]. Monday.

Our entire corps marched to Sobohleben, but our regiment remained at its bivouacs in Teplitz, where the Imperial Quarters is still located.

27 August [8 September]. Wednesday.

Our battalion was on guard duty in Teplitz. I went there to serve as the head of guards for 24 hours.

---

[62] The regiment lost some 900 killed and wounded.

29 August [10 September]. Friday.

General Wittgenstein's corps moved forward to Pirna, where he encountered Napoleon's entire army and was forced to retreat to Kulm; by four o'clock in the afternoon we heard cannon and musket fire. In the evening, our regiment marched to Sobohleben, but before we could arrive there, we were ordered to turn back and retake our positions at Teplitz. However, we were not allowed to undress since the enemy skirmisher line advanced along the mountain ridge that was located to the left of us.

30 August [11 September]. Saturday.

The French withdrew during the night. All of our regimental officers gathered in Teplitz in the morning to congratulate the Emperor on the occasion of his Name Day.[63] In the evening we held a prayer service at the camp. General Miloradovich tied the St. George ribbons to our flags until we received the St. George flags as a reward for the battle of Kulm.[64]

I was thrilled to receive a letter from St. Petersburg since it has been a very long time since I have received any correspondence. The retreat of the enemy gave us hope that we would be allowed to sleep free but, at about 8 o'clock in the evening, some movements were observed in the woods and orders were issued to double outposts and to sleep fully clothed and with arms in hands.

Deployed at its position at Teplitz, our regiments protected the Imperial Quarters and sent out sentries to guard our Sovereign, and the King of Prussia, alternating this responsibility with the Prussian Guard. Meantime, the Emperor of Austria was always protected by the Austrian grenadiers.

31 August [12 September]. Sunday.

Despite all the anxiety the day before, we had a rather quite night. At 4 o'clock in the afternoon, our batteries at Sobohleben suddenly opened fire, followed by the battalions of the first line. Not knowing what was going on, we were convinced that the battle was about to commence but instead soon received a report that saluted the victory won by the Swedish

---

[63] A name day was a holiday celebrating the day of the year associated with one's given name.

[64] The St. George flags carried inscriptions "For Exploits Demonstrated in the Battle at Kulm on 17 August 1813."

Crown Prince [Bernadotte] over the French at Wittenberg. Some 8000 prisoners and 60 guns fell into the victor's hands. We naturally did not miss a chance to convey this news to the French who were standing in front of us: we sent a messenger to tell them not to worry when they hear the sound of gunfire [since we were celebrating a victory]. This stunt was quite in the spirit of the French. In the evening we heard a musket fire on the wooded hill to our left but otherwise we were not bothered.

SEPTEMBER

3[15] September. Wednesday.

Today I had to travel to Teplitz for 24 hours since I was appointed head of the sentries. While there, I enjoyed the hospitality of [Colonel Yakov] Lamsdorf, His Majesty's flugel-adjutant and an old friend of mine.

While on duty, we always dine with the palace commandant, but we are never given separate rooms and the only refuge to which we are entitled is the guardhouse [*hauptwache*]. Therefore, we always try to find a place with one of our acquaintances at the Imperial Quarters. However, the dinner with the palace commandant is always pleasant, firstly, because we are well fed, and secondly, we can always hear fresh news from various eminent people who dine with us. The Emperor usually dines with Count Arakcheyev and Tolstoy, and the rest of his suite eats at the palace commandant's quarters. It was at one of these dinners that I [met and] listened to the famous defector Lt. Gen. [Henri] Jomini. The Emperor appointed him as his adjutant-general, but did not give him any actual command. Jomini claimed that Napoleon's army was full of robbers and that one cannot imagine the full scale of disorders that overtook it.

4[16] September. Thursday.

I slept like a dead until 7 am. Lamsdorf's apartment is incomparably more convenient than a tent, where I had to return after the changing of the guard.

5[17] September. Friday.

After lunch I went to our corps to see Nikolai. These gentlemen [the Life Guard Lithuanian Regiment] was deployed between Teplitz and Sobohleben. They received an order to be ready for battle but at Teplitz we were still unaware of any such orders. The cannonade kept coming closer and it seemed that our advance guard was retreating. However, upon returning to our camp, I learned that our troops captured 12 guns and 2000 French prisoners. The captured [French] general [Kleizer] told us that two [French] corps will attack us tomorrow.

6[18] September. Saturday.

During the Saturday night, the Austrian and Prussian troops moved forward without halting anywhere and, by morning, they formed the first line. By 9 o'clock the enemy attacked Hellendorf, but by noon our troops occupied the village and remained peacefully there for the rest of the day.

7[19] September. Sunday.

As a duty officer, I spent the whole day in Teplitz. The French retreated beyond Peterswalde. Our advance guard was ordered no to advance too far forward to avoid falling into an ambush. At night I went to see Pushkin and Zybin.

8[20] September. Monday.

I accepted my hosts' request to spend another night with them.

9[21] September. Friday.

My roommates Brinken and Khrapovitskii found a large manor house located behind our bivouac. They settled there since house was abandoned by its owners. Upon returning from the town [and hearing the news] I moved in with them.

General Moreau, who lost both his legs during the battle near Dresden, has died in Prague.

I had an opportunity to read several letters from the French army that had been intercepted during last few days. They all attest to disorders and despair reigning in Napoleon's army.

10[22] September. Wednesday.

Before lunch I went to Schteibad, which is located near Teplitz. The water is as good as in the city and I took great pleasure in swimming there.

11[23] September. Thursday.

I dined with Zybin in Teplitz. Count Arakcheyev, seeing me in the street and wanting to please me, told me that on the 15th I will receive a golden sword for my actions at [the battle of] Kulm. However, General Potemkin promised me to procure a golden sword with a 2,000 ruble pension for me so I was upset to hear that I was to receive just a golden sword, especially since some young officers, sub-lieutenants who have not even sniffed the gunpowder, were nominated for the same award, while Colonel Nabokov, just one year senior that me, was nominated to promotion to the rank of major general. I was deeply offended by such injustice.

12[24] September. Friday.

My disappointment did not prevent me from sleeping well, and I woke up in a better mood this morning. All my colleagues are well aware how I carried out my duties [at Kulm] and they all are of the opinion that I was wronged. For me, this is a greater reward than any possible order. So such support completely reassured me, and I recovered my good spirits.

14[26] September. Sunday.

I was in Teplitz. Count Arakcheyev asked me to stay for a lunch; this was a very special favor. There were only three of us: the count, his physician and me. This is clearly a sign of friendship.

15[27] September. Monday.

The day began a solemn liturgy. The Emperor and King of Prussia attended the service in the church. After leaving the service I went to Nicolai so we could go to a luncheon that was organized by the Russian Guard in honor of the Prussian Guard. This feast took place in a large barracks built specifically for this occasion. The Emperor, King of Prussia, the young princes and their entire entourage all honored this celebration with their presence. Our friendship with the Prussians grew stronger. But an accident almost overshadowed the entire event. A fire broke out in the house next to the barracks just as our most august guests were dining. Our immediate concern was for the safety of the sacred heads and as soon as they were out of danger, we rushed back to save dishes since the kitchen was located inside the burning house. Everything ended as we desired. The barracks was untouched and most dishes were saved, but when our guests departed and we turned to eat, we realized that in our concern for the safety of our honorable guests, we have ignored our own food and consequently had to settle for a rather poor dinner. I returned home at 7 pm.

16[28] September. Tuesday.

People talks about the impending departure but since no orders have been issued yet, I took an opportunity to bathe in Schteibad once more.

17[29] September. Wednesday.

An order to depart was issue in the morning but it was countermanded and we remained on the ground.

18[30] September. Thursday.

At last, after a month long rest, we broke up our camp and departed. The Emperor reviewed our corps in Sobohleben, and then our regiment in Teplitz. Our regiment joined the corps in the afternoon when it passed through Teplitz. We marched through Dux to Brick, where we bivouacked.

19-22 September [1-4 October]. Friday through Monday.

We remained on the ground, spending time in Brick, avoiding staying inside a tent because of very damp weather.

23 September [5 October]. Tuesday.

Our corps departed at 9 am, marching from Brick to Komotau. Muddy road and rain made this day unbearable for us. And to top it off, we were ordered to remain constantly ready for battle, which kept us in a stressed out throughout the day.

24-26 September [6-8 October]. Wednesday - Friday.

We remained at the camp near Komotau. A great uncertainty reigned everywhere. We were told to prepare for departure several times but after some rational thinking it was finally decided to leave us alone. We held solemn prayers to celebrate victory gained by General Blucher between Torgau and Wittenberg, where he and his army, which is called the Silesian Army, drove the enemy to the left bank of the Elbe River.[65]

27 September [9 October]. Saturday.

Our corps marched out at 5 am. It proceeded through Sebastianburg to Marienberg, where we bivouacked. The weather is horrible. This is the third time we have entered Saxony.

28 September [10 October]. Sunday.

We marched through Zschopau to Chemnitz, where we arrived very late in the day because we departed only at noon. It rains incessantly. During our halt at Zschopau , I had the opportunity to admire the picturesque location of this small town. It is located a charming valley irrigated by the small Zschopau River.

29 September [11 October]. Monday.

We departed at 9 am, passed through Chemnitz towards Penig, where we set up our camp. Chemnitz is a large beautiful city. [Sadly] I stayed only for a short time there, just enough to have a breakfast.

30 September [12 October]. Tuesday.

Our corps resumed its march between 8 and 9 am, crossed the Mulde River at Penig and proceeded on a country road towards Altenburg, where we bivouacked. It was already a sunset when we finally stopped. I immediately went with several officers to Altenburg, where we ordered a dinner at the tavern called "Deer" and took a walk around the city while waiting for dinner.

Altenburg is the main city of the Altenburg Principality which forms a part of the Duchy of Saxe-Gotha. This is the largest city in Saxony after Dresden. It is very well laid out and has two squares.

After dinner it was too late to go back to our camp so we decided to spend the night in the city.

---

[65] Pushin refers to the battle of Wartenberg fought on 6 October 1813.

OCTOBER

1[13] October. Wednesday.

Still at our camp near Altenburg. [After spending the night in town] we were awakened at 6 o'clock in the morning and, without wasting any time, we immediately returned to the camp. After confirming that we were not departing today, we then returned to Altenburg, where we again remained until night.

There is wonderful castle of Gothic architecture, situated on a hill on the edge of town. There is also a church, quite spacious and famous for its organs. The organist, a talented musician, delighted us by demonstrating his talents.

2[14] October. Thursday.

The corps departed from its camp at Altenburg at 8 o'clock in the morning. It marched towards Mozelwitz where it bivouacked for the night.

3[15] October. Friday.

We marched out at 1 pm. Our corps proceeded through Lukau to Audigast, a village located northwest[66] of Pegau and very close to that city. The Emperor caught up with at Lukau, where local population greeted him enthusiastically.

4[16] – 7[19] October. Saturday - Tuesday.

Decisive battle at Leipzig. We left out camp at Audigast at 7 pm on Saturday. Our corps marched to Rotha and, after passing through this town, it deployed in battle formation and moved towards Leipzig, proceeding on the road from Borna and keeping the Pleisse River on its left.

At 10 o'clock the corps took up positions between Rotha and Leipzig. Not all Allied armies had arrived there yet while Napoleon had all his forces gathered together. Our cavalry was pushed back by 4 pm, suffering

---

[66] Pushin is probably mistaken since modern-day town of Audigast is located northeast of Pegau.

heavy losses, including [Lieutenant-]General [Ivan] Shevich who commanded the Guards hussars.[67] To avert the immediate danger [to our retreating cavalrymen], our columns were moved forward and three hundred Guards Cossacks, who formed the Emperor's escort, charged at the enemy's cavalry, and halted its pursuit of our cavalry. The Guard infantry remained under arms and showered by enemy cannonball until the nightfall. The Life Guard Jager and Finland Regiments took a very active part in the battle. We all spent the night on the battlefield in expectation that the enemy gun, which stopped firing only at night, would awake us in the morning.

I cannot fail to mention one little fact regarding Count Arakcheyev, which took place around 5 pm today. When our cavalry was thrown back and our columns advanced in battle order to stop enemy attack, the Emperor and his entire suite remained behind our lines. While the Guard Cossacks were deploying for their dashing charge, Count Arakcheyev left the [Emperor's entourage] and approached the battalion, where I served. He called me up and started a friendly conversation. Just at that moment French batteries closest to us opened fire and one of their grenades exploded just 50 paces from the count. He was surprised by its sound since he had never heard it before in his life. Stopping mid-sentence, he asked me what it was. "A grenade," I replied, ready to resume our suddenly interrupted conversation, but upon hearing the word "grenade" the count's face changed, he quickly turned his horse and swiftly galloped away from such a dangerous place, leaving me in a rather embarrassing position. His adjutant Kleinmichel, who accompanied the count, simply shrugged his shoulders when the count fled and spurred his horse to follow him.[68] That same day my old roommate Prince Sergei Trubetskoy was wounded in the thigh.

5, 6 and 7 [17-19] October. Sunday - Tuesday.

I was very surprised to wake up rather late in the morning and in the same place. In fact, our corps did not move for an entire day. The French made no attempts to attack us and instead spent the day preparing for battle. All our armies gathered together in the valleys of Leipzig. The army of the Crown Prince of Sweden [Bernadotte] and the army of General Bennigsen moved to the first line and took up positions on the right flank. On Monday, at 10 o'clock, we attacked the French with superior

---

[67] Shevich commanded the Guard Light Cavalry Division.

[68] Pushin later added a comment on the margins: Returning to St. Petersburg, I was careless enough to mention this incident to the count's mistress Ms. Pukalova, and ever since I found myself in disgrace.

forces. They were completely destroyed and none of their cannonballs reached us while we stood in reserve. When we were ordered to attack, we moved forward without firing. But the same cannot be said of others, who suffered heavily. The French fought fiercely, especially around the village of Konnewitz which they defended to cover their retreat since they no longer fought to win but to escape. The fighting ended with nightfall. Our corps spent the night in close proximity to Konnewitz.

During the Tuesday night the enemy moved out all of his outposts between the city of Leipzig and our lines, and at daybreak his rearguard was attacked at the gates and on the outskirts of the city. Since our support was no longer necessary, our corps was ordered to move to Pegau while I - having no battalion to command since out of three battalions we managed to form only two – decided to visit Leipzig. I entered the city with leading columns of our troops, who routed Napoleon's rear guard; [the French] army was in full retreat. The city residents greeted us enthusiastically and expressed genuine joy at seeing us. I spent considerable time wandering through the streets of the city and enjoying cordial reception shown to us.

The king of Saxony, who continues to be faithful to Napoleon, has been declared a prisoner of war. Despite the occupation of his kingdom, he never desired to join the Alliance. The French Marshal Prince Poniatowski, who commanded Napoleon's rear guard, was killed in the morning. He was the last hope of Poland.

Thus, the French army has been destroyed for the second time.

I left Leipzig in the late afternoon and reached Zwenkau by evening. I was fortunate to find a dinner there since I have not eaten anything for an entire day. I then went to Pegau, where we arrived late at night.

8[20] October. Wednesday.

Our corps marched out at noon. [In the evening] we bivouacked at Teuchern.

9[21] October. Thursday.

We departed at 7 am. [By nightfall] our bivouacs were at Naumburg. This is a very large town.

10[22] October. Friday.

Our corps departed from its bivouacs at Naumburg at noon, crossed the Saal River at [Bad] Kössen and then proceeded to Hassenhausen, where we set up our camp.

The crossing of the Saal considerably delayed the movement of our columns, so I went to Kössen and spent the night at a local farmer's house.

11[23] October. Saturday.

I woke up at 5 am and quickly rejoined our Corps, which still remained at Hassenhausen, gathered on the road to Eckartsberga. At noon it marched through Aurstedt towards Oberreissen, a village on the border of Saxe-Weimar, where we bivouacked.

12[24] October. Sunday.

Our corps departed at 9 am and entered the territory of Saxe-Weimar. Marching on country roads, we passed very close from Weimar and proceeded towards the main road that ran from this city to Erfurt. The corps halted at Ulla, while the battalion where I am listed, was assigned to the village of Gaberndorf, where it occupied apartments.

13[25] October. Monday.

I spent the entire day in Weimar. I greatly enjoyed the theater, which staged the opera "Doktor und Apotheker"[69] which was superbly performed. The aged Duchess of Weimar and numerous princes were in attendance, all sitting in the Duchess's booth. During the intermission, they drank tea. The city of Weimar, in effect, is just a poorly fortified small town, but despite this I spent the entire day there and left only late in the evening to return to Gaberndorf.

14[26] October. Tuesday.

The day began with a solemn liturgy and prayer service in gratitude for the victory won at Leipzig. After the parade our corps marched through [Bad] Berka and Tannroda to Kranichfeld, where we bivouacked. We

---

[69] This opera, composed by August Carl Ditters von Dittersdorf (1739 – 1799), one of the leading Austrian composers of the 18th century, enjoyed a tremendous success in his lifetime, playing in theaters all over Europe.

arrived there late in the day since bad weather, mountainous terrain and, finally, darkness greatly complicated our movement.

15[27] October. Wednesday.

Our corps marched to Arnstadt, where we bivouacked just before sunset. Arnstadt belongs to Prince Schwartzenberg and it is a large and well built town. I spent the evening there.

16[28] October. Thursday.

Our corps departed at 8 am. We marched for the entire day on a country road, entering the Thuringian Forest and walking in a very mountainous terrain. We finally bivouacked around midnight near the village of Mehlis, north-east of Zepau. When we departed from our position at Arnstadt, I went to eat breakfast in town and came across Saxon king's adjutant, who escaped from the French at Erfurt. He was very surprised to hear that the King considered himself as a prisoner of the Allied sovereigns at the time when his own people were their ally. We are now in the territory of Saxe-Gotha.

17[29] October. Friday.

The corps marched out at 9 am. [By the end of the day] out troops were billeted in apartments. Our regiment is at Kundorf while the corps headquarters is at Schwarz.

We are now in the duchy of Duchy of Saxe-Meiningen.

Local commoners wear shirts [*bluzy*] while women wear cardboard cuirasses [probably a corset].

18[30] October. Saturday.

The day of rest.

19 October [31 October]. Sunday.

We departed at 8 o'clock in the morning and entered the archduchy of Würzburg. The corps headquarters went to Oberstren, a village on the road from Mellrichstadt, and took quarters at Mittelstreu.

20 October [1 November]. Monday.

We marched at 8 o'clock in the morning. The Imperial Quarters moved to Munnerstadt, the corps headquarters is in Popenlauer, while our regiment is in apartments in Reichenbach.

21 October [2 November]. Tuesday.

We moved out at 7 am. The Corps headquarters went to Euerbach, while the Second Battalion, which I now command, proceeded to Rutschenhausen [about three miles from Euerbach]. Of the three battalion commanders who served at Kulm, [Colonel Andrei] Yefimovich has been killed, while Nabokov and Posnikov have been promoted to major generals.

Since the 19th we have been moving on the territory of the archduchy we Wurtzburg and, quartering with local peasants, we have observed that they do not live as prosperously as the population of other provinces of Saxony, and aside from the abundance of wine, they lack many other necessities. There are no candles in houses, yet there are *ploshki*[70] everywhere. Rumors claim that we will soon stop in Frankfurt [on Maine].

22 October [3 November]. Wednesday.

We had a very long march today. My battalion moved from Rutschenhausen through Woermann [?] to Guntersleben, where we took up quarters.[71]

23 October [4 November]. Thursday.

The day of rest, though not for my battalion, which, like the 3rd Battalion, has been ordered to march to Thungersheim, a village located on the right bank of the River Main, about three quarters of a [Russian] mile from Guntersleben. One cannot imagine a more picturesque countryside than the one we passed today on our short march. These hills, covered with vineyards, this Main River flowing at their bottom and watering the beautiful Thungersheim valley captivate the attention of not only us, the natives of the North, but even the inhabitants of places with much more favorable climates. It is difficult to convey the impression all

---

[70] Ploshki was a clay bowl with a wicker and filled with melted tallow.

[71] Presently, Rutschenhausen is about 26 miles away from Guntersleben.

of this had on us. The village of Thungersheim deserves the name of a city when compared to some settlements in Russia and Poland, which have been called towns for no apparent reason.

24 October [5 November]. Friday.

We marched out at 9 am. My battalion, having crossed the Main River twice, occupied quarters at Trendelf, about ¼ [Russian] mile away from Hamburg [?]. Our corps headquarters also moved to this village. Because my roommates are listed in the 3rd Battalion, which stopped at another village, I found myself all alone and my apartment felt rather solitary.

25 October [6 November]. Saturday.

We marched on the road to Aschaffenburg, and halted on its outskirts, taking quarters at Grunmorsbach. We are already in Franconia, the possession of the Prince Primate.[72]

26 October [7 November]. Sunday.

We passed through Aschaffenburg, a very beautiful city, where our troops crossed the Main once more. Our regiment then marched to Kleinostheim, where we took up our new quarters. In Aschaffenburg there is a wonderful castle that belongs to the Prince Primate.

The village of Kleinostheim is vast and people say that there was a considerable town once but it was destroyed by a fire. In one of the squares, there are still three houses and one tree that survived the fire. The community gathered around the tree to discuss issues relating to the restoration of the homes following the disaster.

27 October [8 November]. Monday.

Despite the fact that Frankfurt was still 8 hours away, we received orders to put on our full parade uniforms. It was raining incessantly and we were rather upset that upon entering Frankfurt we would make soiled and unpleasant appearance. To our joy, the order was soon cancelled and we were told to take up quarters at Offenbach, the capital of Prince

---

[72] Pushin refers to Karl Dalberg, Archbishop-Elector of Mainz, Arch-Chancellor of the Holy Roman Empire, Prince of Regensburg, Primate of the Confederation of the Rhine and Grand-Duke of Frankfurt.

Issenburg's domain, located just ¾ [Russian] mile west of Frankfurt on Main.

28 October [9 November]. Tuesday.

Day of rest at Offenbach. This town produces very nice carriages but there is nothing else noteworthy here. I lodged with a tailor and amused myself by flirting with Elizabeth Sperl, my host's wife's cousin.

29 October [10 November]. Wednesday.

We made a triumphant and solemn entrance into Frankfurt, passing through the suburbs of Sachsenhausen and crossing on the bridge that separates the city and the suburbs. We then paraded in front of the both Emperors [Alexander and Francis] who have arrived to the barrier to greet us.

I was billeted in an apartment belonging to some Hoerster, whose family consisted of his mother-in-law Mrs. Terinasi and wife Marianne. They welcomed and treated me very well, but this did not prevent me from concluding that Ms. Terinasi is just an old hag, gossiper and grouch. In the evening Mr. Hoerster invited me to his theater box to attend a play. The theater auditorium was pretty good, performers – average and orchestra - good. They staged the opera "The Caliph of Baghdad"[73] in German.

30 October [11 November]. Thursday.

The rain prevented me from exploring the city as I intended it but in the evening I managed to attend the theater again, this time it was [Mozart's] "Don Juan".

31 October [12 November]. Friday.

Mr. Hoerster was kind enough to accompany me on a tour of the city. Frankfurt is surrounded by a boulevard, which is crowded with people in good weather. There is a monument to the Prince of Hesse, who was killed during the capture of Frankfurt. The bridge over the Main River, which I previously mentioned, is very beautiful but it cannot be compared to that in Dresden. Not far from the bridge there is a cathedral where the monarchs are crowned.

---

[73] This was a comedy written by French composer François-Adrien Boïeldieu.

NOVEMBER

1 [13] November. Saturday.

In this country it is customary to eat potatoes on Saturdays, which I regretted very much today. Similarly, the feast of St.. Martin on 11 November (October 30) is commemorated by eating a goose. I attended the opera "Cendrillon" today.[74]

2 [14] November. Sunday.

We held a major parade to mark the arrival of the King of Prussia in Frankfurt. Austrian troops were also under arms, but everyone praised us more. After lunch, I traveled to Offenbach. Nicholas was there, as well as Lisa Sperl, with whom I am in a very close relationship.

4 [16] November. Tuesday.

I attended a ball at the theater. I went there with Mr. Hoerster and stayed until dinner, when we returned home. This event was noteworthy for numerous royals who attended it: there were Russian and Austrian rulers, kings of Prussia and Bavaria, the Grand Duke Constantine Pavlovich, the princes of Oldenburg, Corburg, Darmstadt, Sweden, the families of the Prussian, Bavarian and other rulers.

5 [17] November. Wednesday.

After lunch I went to Offenbach to spend some time with Mlle Sperl and returned home only late in the evening.

11 [23] November. Tuesday.

The Emperor's sisters Grand Duchesses Maria Pavlovna and Ekaterina Pavlovna, the former being the Grand Duchess of Weimar and the latter – of Oldenburg,[75] have arrived today in Frankfurt.

---

[74] The Cendrillon opera was written by the Maltese-born composer Nicolas Isouard.

[75] Maria Pavlovna was married to Charles Frederick, Grand Duke of Saxe-Weimar-Eisenach. Ekaterina Pavlovna was married to Duke George of Oldenburg, the second son

21 November [3 December]. Friday.

Today is our regiment's holiday, which we first celebrated with a solemn liturgy, and then received congratulations from the Emperor, our regimental chef, at the Roten Haus. All the monarchs and princes of blood, as well as all staff officers from our corps, have been invited.

23 November [5 December]. Sunday.

Mr. Hoerster's father lives in Darmstadt so we decided to visit him today. Madame Marianne, her husband and I sat in a two-seat carriage, drawn only by a pair of horses which would have seemed very strange in Russia. We traveled for about three [Russian] miles. About half way there,[76] we stopped at Langen to drink a bottle of wine and eat a piece of cheese while horses rested. Continuing our journey, we arrived at Darmstadt around 3 pm and the old man and his large family were already waiting for us for lunch. As soon as we finished eating, the sun had set and prevented us from exploring the city before the [theater] play. So postponed sightseeing till tomorrow and satisfied my curiosity by examining the theater. Today they staged the opera *Zampa ou La fiancée de marbre*, which caused a furor in Darmstadt. In support of the citizens of this city, I must confess that I found this opera containing too many changes of scenery and neither music, nor theater or actors pleased me. But tastes, of course, differ, and should not be argued about, so this is just my opinion. The Frankfurt Theater is superior to the Darmstadt one, which is smaller in size. The court of the Duke [Ludwig] of Hesse-Darmstadt attended the opera. The Crown Prince was in a separate box to the left of the ducal box, while the duke's mistress, who apparently wields some influence, was in another small box to the right from the duke. She is just an actress, Madame Frank but the Duchess herself is forced to treat her very circumspectly. After the opera we went back to the old man Hoerster for supper and sleep.

24 November [6 December]. Monday.

---

of the ruling Duke Peter of Oldenburg. Her husband passed away in late 1812 from typhoid fever. She later married Crown Prince William of Wurttemberg, whom she married in 1816.

[76] Nowadays, Darmstadt is about 26 km [17 miles] away from Frankfurt while Langen is about 13 km [8.5 miles].

As soon as we finished drinking coffee, the young Hoerster took me into the city, wanting to show me all the sights. The ancient town is rather small; the new town, although not larger, is well built and its streets are broad and regular; the main square is surrounded by very beautiful buildings, which attract the attention of foreign visitors. This is the first German city that I can compare with St. Petersburg. Exerzierhaus[77] is remarkable for its size, and it served as a model for the first exerzierhaus built in Russia. The arsenal contains nothing particularly interesting. The art gallery in the old Duke's castle deserves a visit, but I could not get there. Judging by its exterior, the castle belongs to Gothic architecture and is surrounded by a moat; one part of the castle is uninhabited. After sightseeing, we went back to the old man Hoerster, bid farewell to him and his family and returned to Frankfurt in the same manner as we came to Darmstadt. We had the same meager breakfast in Langen as before, and by noon, we were already at home, where Madame Terinasi was already waiting for us with lunch.

27 November [9 December]. Thursday.

General Uvarov gave a wonderful ball at the Roten Haus. The hall was beautifully decorated and numerous guests assembled there. I stayed at the ball until 9 pm and returned home for dinner.

29 November [11 December]. Saturday.

Because of great inconvenience of constantly traveling to Offenbach to see my beautiful Mlle Sperl, I agreed to her offer to settle her in Frankfurt. But as soon as I arranged an apartment for her, she, without my permission for it, began telling everyone that she was my wife. I was very upset to hear this but this blunder was made possible because she received permission to leave Offenbach only because she passed herself as my wife. So I had to decide: either to lose a lover or not to publicize her lie. I chose to remain silent, especially since I personally did not deceive the [municipal] authorities of Offenbach – I made no verbal or written request to anyone and Mlle Sperl did everyone herself, in fact without my knowledge of. So I scolded her for this ploy but rented a small apartment for her in Frankfurt and visited her every day.

Today I received an order to depart [towards the Rhine River] tomorrow. In the evening I went to see my beauty for the last time and

---

[77] Military barracks where soldiers were trained.

not daring to tell her about my departure, I said goodbye with a heavy heart and returned home to enjoy last supper with my hosts.

30 November [12 December]. Sunday.

Our regiment departed at 9 am on the Darmstadt road and bivouacked not far from this city, at a place called Arheilgen. As soon as we arrived there, I was told that [upon our departure from Frankfurt] a very beautiful and exquisitely dressed woman had approached General [Mikhail] Miloradovich on the main road and asked him to assist her in finding me. The General, a very gallant man, slightly teased this gorgeous petitioner and then offered her his personal carriage, in which she arrived to the corps headquarters. I immediately realized that it was none other than Mlle Liza Sperl so I dispatched an orderly, who attended my luggage, to the corps headquarters with instructions to bring this woman to me. He deftly accomplished this assignment and Liza Sperl was soon in my arms. She beseeched me to take her with me and I could not refuse her. So we settled down together as a husband and wife. Back in Offenbach she waited on me at her cousin tailor's dinner table while now she was sitting with me at the same table.

DECEMBER

1 [13] December. Monday.

Today we held a parade in Darmstadt but because on such occasions our regiment was usually formed in two battalions due to the lack of manpower, I, as the youngest of the three battalion commanders, ended up without a battalion. I decided to take advantage of this and paid a visit to the old man Hoerster, drank coffee with him and then caught up with the regiment at it was marching to Zwingenberg, where we arrived very late in the evening. At this point, my battalion (and one battalion) moved off the main road, turned left and marched for about one mile in this direction to take up quarters at Reichenbach. Liza Sperl traveled with our luggage in a carriage that I obtained for her and I found her with an already cooked meal in Reichenbach.

2 [14] December. Tuesday.

A day of rest in Reichenbach. My batman Luka fell ill and begged me to let him go to Frankfurt to be treated. I took the opportunity to convince Mlle Sperk to return home with Luka. This proved to be not as easy as I anticipated and I had to use all my eloquence to persuade my beloved mistress to go home. Only through my promise that she could return to me with Luka was I able to overcome her stubbornness, and it was decided that just as we march forward, she will return to Frankfurt with Luka.

3 [15] December. Wednesday.

We marched at 7 am. I parted with Mlle Sperk as we agreed upon the day before.

We marched through Bensheim, Heppenheim and Weinheim to Schriesheim, where our regiment took up quarters. Our corps headquarters is located in Weinheim.

4 [16] December. Thursday.

We crossed the Neckar River in Heidelberg. The corps headquarters is in Leimen while we are in Walldorf.

We are in a beautiful countryside and the picturesque views that we admired during today's marching reveals the proximity of the charming Switzerland. The view of the old town of Heidelberg from the bridge over the Neckar River is simply breathtaking. This city has university, and a barrel of an incredible size.[78]

5 [17] December. Friday.

We departed at 8 am, marching through Bruchsal to Buchenau, where our regiment took up quarters.

6 [18] December. Saturday.

According to our marching schedule, we were supposed to be having a day of rest today but instead we were told that we had to take up quarters in the vicinity of Durlach since we were very close from it.

Marching with my battalion at 8 o'clock in the morning, I went to Weingarten, from where our entire regiment proceeded to Grotzingen,

---

[78] The famous Heidelberg Tun (Großes Fass) is a vast wine vat in the cellars of Heidelberg Castle. There have been four such barrels in the history of Heidelberg and the one that Pushin refers to was made in 1751 and has a capacity of approximately 220,000 litres (58,100 U.S. gallons).

the village about half a mile north from Durlach. We are supposed to spend the night here so we can arrive in Karlsruhe just in time for tomorrow's parade.

7 [19] December. Sunday.

I do not participate in today's parade for the reason I have already mentioned above. I stayed at home until the end of the parade in Karlsruhe and the return of my regiment to Grotzingen.

8 [20] December. Monday.

I marched with my battalion at 9 am. Two companies were billeted at Palmbach, and the other two are at Wolfartsweier; the former village is at a distance of half an hour's walk from Durlach. I am billeted with the village pastor. All officers spent the day with me and since we found a piano and guitar, not to mention cards, at my apartment, we quickly took up playing music and cards for the rest of the day, without noticing how quickly time flew by. Although our stay in Frankfurt was noisier, the stay in Palmbach strengthened our camaraderie.

9 [21] December. Tuesday.

I went to Karlsruhe, which is just 2 hours away from us. First of all, I did some shopping and then went to dine at the Darmstadt tavern, which fully satisfied me. After lunch I spent time walking around the city, but because time was short and I had to think about returning to Palmbach, I limited myself to only a superficial examination of the city. The castle and especially the park are superb. Alleys are as wide and beautiful as city streets and as straight as a line. Karlsruhe and its proper planning remind me of St. Petersburg more than Darmstadt.

17 [29] December. Wednesday.

More than a week has passed since we have arrived here but our daily life has become so monotonous that there is nothing to write about in my diary. All officers usually gather at my place and entertain themselves with music and playing cards, just as they did on the first day of our arrival here. I left my quarters just once to attend a lunch with General Potemkin. We should depart tomorrow so I think it necessary to give an idea what Palmbach is. This is a French colony, full of immigrants who fled from their homeland by the Edict of Nantes.[79] All old people speak

French and German, but prefer the latter. Apparently, malevolence is so hard to forget that after such long period of time these people hate even the language of their persecutors, even though it had once been their native dialect.

18 [30] December. Thursday.

Our corps was ordered to go to Rastatt, but because all generals and staff officers were invited to dinner at the Grand Duke, I ordered my battalion to start marching while I went to Karlsruhe. Along the way I admired a poplar alley that was adjacent to the main road from Durlach to Karlsruhe. The trees are of incredible height. The dinner at Grand Duke of Baden['s estate][80] was excellent, and the etiquette more stringent than in St. Petersburg. Apparently these little ruling princes want to make sure that people do not forget that they are princes, and therefore they constantly remind about their titles and organize events with as much pomp and splendor as possible to dazzle the common people. The palace in Karlsruhe is small but beautifully furnished and decorated.

We gathered in one of the front rooms. When several generals arrived, we were moved into a different room, and when General Miloradovich arrived, we were moved to still another room, where the Grand Duke received us. His wife, the Duchess Stephanie Napoleon[81] came after him, accompanied by two ladies who were as ugly as the Duchess herself was beautiful.

It is very likely that the adopted daughter of the French Emperor was not particularly thrilled to see us, but had to pretend and hide her true feelings. She was very charming and gracious with us. Her uneasiness did not last long because when we were invited to the table, she retired to her apartments and the Grand Duke stayed alone with us. After dinner, I mounted my horse and rode through Ettlingen and Rastatt to catch up with my battalion, which was billeted in Oos [Ooser].[82]

---

[79] The Edict of Nantes was issued by King Henry IV in 1598 granting the Calvinist Protestants of France substantial rights in a nation still considered essentially Catholic. The edict provoked a negative reaction among the devout Catholics and Pushin seems to suggest that the French immigrants in Palmbach were Protestants who were persecuted following the Edict.

[80] The duke was Karl Ludwig Friedrich, who ruled Baden since 1811.

[81] Stéphanie Louise Adrienne de Beauharnais was related to Alexandre, Vicomte de Beauharnais (first cousin of her father) who was married to Joséphine Tascher de la Pagerie, who later married Napoleon. During the First Empire, Napoleon extended his patronage to Stephanie, whom he adopted and married to the Grand Duke of Baden in July 1806. By most accounts the arranged marriage was not particularly successful.

19 [31] December. Friday.

We departed at 8 o'clock in the morning. The corps headquarters moved to Achern, while I proceeded with my battalion to Önsbach. As we approached Achern on the main road that run from Rastatt, we received General Miloradovich's command to move by a ceremonial march in front of the monument erected on the spot where the great Turenne had been killed. The people still show the cannonball that killed him.[83]

20 December [1 January 1814]. Saturday.

The corps headquarters went to Offenburg while we moved further to Ortenberg. When the regiment was passing through Offenburg, I left the unit to have a lunch since I had not eaten anything since 9 am. But I was served a miserable lunch at the tavern "Sonne" and I must say that the rest of the town is not particularly appealing either.

21 December [2 January]. Sunday.

Day of rest in Ortenberg.

22 December [3 January]. Monday.

The corps headquarters has been moved to Mahlberg while our regiment made a lengthy march to Ettenheim.

23 December [4 January]. Tuesday.

The Main Headquarters has been set up at Emmendingen while I was deployed with two companies of my battalion at Kollmarsreute. Today we passed through the towns of Herbolzheim and Kenzingen that I mention just to indicate the direction of our march [along France's frontier on the Rhine] because they, like many other small towns that so abound in Germany, do not represent anything noteworthy.

---

[82] Ooser is about 24 miles [37 km] away from Karlsruhe.

[83] Henri de la Tour d'Auvergne-Bouillon, the Vicomte de Turenne, one of the best generals of Kings Louis XIII and Louis XIV. He earned the title of the Marshal of France before being mortally wounded at the battle of Salzbach (Sasbach) on 27 July 1675.

24 December [5 January]. Wednesday.

In order to get closer to Freiburg, where we are supposed to attend a parade, I marched with my battalion to Umkirch, a village located ¾ mile north-east of Freiburg.

25 December [6 January]. Thursday.

Day of rest. First thing in the morning I went to congratulate General Potemkin with the holiday, and then went to Freiburg, where the Emperor's Quarters have been set up. I gave a letter addressed to Madame B. to Count Arakcheyev, who still remains my faithful friend. Unfortunately, things are not as well in my relationship with Madame B., who has started to write less and less. I think somebody told her about my adventures with Elizabeth Sperl.

In Freiburg, I examined the great cathedral which is very ancient and rather splendid.[84] By coincidence the King of Prussia was inside the cathedral when I entered it and His Majesty kindly talked to me and invited to accompany him on a tour of this ancient monument. One can imagine how thrilled I was to accept this proposal, not the least because the [local authorities] showed everything more eagerly to the Prussian king than they would have done for me.

Thus, His Majesty and I admired together the "Last Supper" which is exquisitely carved. Each of the thirteen faces has a special expression, revealing the artist's rich imagination. The priestly vestments and the tomb of St. Alexander of Rome are splendid and luxurious. The stained glass in some windows attracts particular attention because the secret of their manufacture is unknown today. After seeing all these gems, I left the cathedral along with the king and, having taken leave of His Majesty, I went to eat at some tavern before returning to Umkirch.

26 December [7 January]. Friday.

We held a grand parade in Freiburg. As usual I was not involved and, having dispatched my battalion to the parade, I rented a peasant wagon to go directly to Staufen [im Breisgau] where our quarters were supposed to move later today. As I drove there, I observed the landscape which is so beautiful in appearance. On the left I could see the Black Forest while on

---

[84] The construction of the Gothic church Freiburg Minster (*Freiburger Münster*), which features a 116 meter tower, had began in the early 13th century and was completed around 1330s.

the right I could discern the Vosges beyond the Rhine. [The area is so picturesque that] at times it seemed that the road ran through a garden. The area is very populated and I encountered numerous villages on my way. However, local residents are poorer, dirtier, and less civilized than in other parts of Germany that I have seen so far. Deep in my thoughts I walked around Staufen without noticing how quickly time passed by. My regiment, however, did not arrive as it was supposed to and I did not know the cause of such a delay. Finally, I received a notice that the regiment halted for the night at Kirchhofen, about an hour away from Staufen. I decided not to join the regiment, and stayed for the night in Staufen, where the Guard Uhlans have already occupied their quarters; Colonel [Alexander] Muller[85] was with them and spent the evening with him.

27 December [8 January]. Saturday.

Early in the day, I dispatched my men directly to Schliengen and then, at 9 am, I mounted my horse and followed the same road in their wake but upon reaching Ober-Weiler [?] I felt so exhausted from traveling on this country road that I decided to get to the main road and therefore went to Mullheim. I caught up with the regiment just as it was passing in front of His Majesty and proceeded with it to Kandern, where the regiment was billeted.

Our reserves have arrived today and my battalion received additional men so from now on I will not be able to avoid the parades. My cousin Nicholas has also arrived with the reserves and I saw him on the march.

28 December [9 January]. Sunday.

Our regiment marched at 9 o'clock in the morning, moving through Lörrach. Upon arriving there, we occupied several villages. My battalion was ordered to Adelhauzen but the short distance from Lörrach to Adelhauzen proved to be rather challenging. We encountered so many hills and had to move so often up and down that there could be no doubt that we were near Switzerland. The countryside is very picturesque but the roads are disgusting. In an area where we currently are located, everything, except for cheese, is worse than in the rest of Germany. Women's clothing is rather diverse; local wear red stockings and tied their hair in front with a black ribbon, which I found quite strange.

---

[85] Muller commanded a squadron of the Life Guard Uhlan Regiment.

29 December [10 January]. Monday.

We remain on the ground. I took advantage of the break to replenish my unit with man from the reserves.

30 December [11 January]. Tuesday.

In anticipation of the review that the entire corps has to undergo upon crossing the Rhine, my regiment received a new disposition that required me to lead my battalion in Hagelberg, which is located further away from Basel than Adelhauzen.

31 December [12 January]. Wednesday.

A day of rest.

THE 1814 CAMPAIGN

JANUARY

1 [12] January. Thursday.

At 8 a.m., I marched with my battalion to reach the place on the main route from Lörrach to Basel where the entire corps was supposed to concentrate. The Badenese Guard has also arrived and joined us for the first time; like the Prussian Guard, it was also attached to our corps. Today was a strong frost, worthy of the sons of the North. Deep snow lay on the ground. By 11 a.m. our entire corps concentrated and waited for the arrival of the Emperor till 2 p.m. His Majesty personally took command of the troops and led them to Basel, which the corps passed in a ceremonial march in front of the Allied monarchs gathered on the main city square.

I do not know if the Swiss were happy to see us but can testify that, for whatever reason, they showed great curiosity upon seeing us. Like an anthill, the streets of Basel were full of people as we passed through the city. After leaving it, we made a bivouac and then moved into the quarters assigned to us. The shortest route led by Huningue, which was still in the French hands and besieged by the Bavarians, so we had to make a long detour to the left. This development made the day extremely tiresome to us. We kept marching till midnight.

Having left Basel, we crossed the border of France to enter the Haute Rhine department, also known as the Old Alsace. After sixteen hours of toiling, my battalion finally reached its bivouac at Nider-Markstadt. The road on which we moved from Basel was horrendous.

2 [14] January. Friday.

Day rest. We were at the distance of only 4 French miles [16.7 km] from Basel; one French mile is equal to 4 Russian verstas.[86] This was the shortest route bypassing Huningue. Assuming that the French would not open fire on a common carriage traveling on the main route, I decided to travel with Captain [Gregory] Yafimovich[87] to Basel to better explore it

---

[86] One versta is equal to 1.06 km or 0.66 mile, so one French mile is equal to 4.24 km.

[87] Yafimovich was Staff Captain of the Life Guard Semeyonovskii Regiment

since we only saw it while passing the day before. Our trip went fine and no one fired upon us. We ate *table d'hôte* in a very cold room.

The Imperial headquarters remained this town so I used this opportunity to mail some letters to St. Petersburg. I then walked in the streets of Basel and, after finding nothing outstanding there, I returned with my companion back to Nider-Markstadt [?] by 8 p.m.

3 [15] January. Saturday.

We marched at 7 am and after a long delay occupied quarters at Hau (Leval), a local village. I hired into my service a local boy Philipp, aged 17 or 18, who is the son of hosts in whose house I was staying and who themselves offered his services to me. This boy seems to be very perceptive and speaks fluently in both French and German, which may turn of great advantage to me in this region.

4 [16] January. Sunday.

I departed with my battalion at 9 a.m. Our regiment marched to Rougemont [de Château] and then further on to take quarters at Lachapelle [-sous-Chaux]. The entire population speaks only on a French dialect. The region is extremely poor.

5 [17] January. Monday.

Today was a very tiresome day. We marched since 7 a.m. till midnight and managed to cover 14 French miles or 56 verstas [59.4 km]. We finally reached the former Franche-Comté, presently known as the Haute Saône. We rested at Lure, where we found a tavern but had a dreadful meal; it is impossible to get any coffee or sugar no matter how much you are willing to pay. The locals meet us very well and wholeheartedly hate Napoleon. The corps headquarters was established at Calmoutier, while we stayed at Villeneuve [La Villeneuve-Bellenoye-et-la-Maize].

6 [18] January. Tuesday.

We marched at 8 a.m. The weather and the road were terrible, a very cold wind blew and the rain poured incessantly. Because of marshy terrain in many places, we often had to move in single file [guskom], especially near Port-sur-Saone, where we crossed the Saone River. The corps headquarters moved to Surgogne, the regimental headquarters was established at Bougy. We thus moved only 7 miles (28 verstas) [29.7 km] in 13 hours. I reached Bougy around 9 p.m., completely wet and chilled to the bones.

7 [19] and 8 [20] January. Wednesday and Thursday.

Standing still.

9 [21] January. Friday.

Our regiment left Bougy at 10 a.m. We moved into Champagne in the Haute Marne department. The corps headquarters was set up at Fayl-Billot while we stopped at Maizières [-sur-Amance]. There are no stoves in this country, only fireplaces. The weather is dry but cold; the Russians, who are accustomed to having stoves back at home, are now freezing in homes in the Champagne.

10 [22] January. Saturday.

Marched at 8 am. The corps headquarters was directed to Orbigny-Au-Val, while I moved with 6 companies to Lavernoy.

11 [23] January. Sunday.

Stayed in place. One of our officers, with a surname of Bock,[88] who, after the battle of Borodino, was considered as a coward by everyone in the regiment, remained a subject of a universal contempt.[89] Although very well educated, this young man was seeking an opportunity to publicly take revenge on those whom he considered his most committed abusers. While staying at Lavernua, he chose a moment when all officers gathered for a lunch at my place. He blatantly showed up at this gathering and loudly denounced two or three of his mortal enemies whom he made out at the meeting. This affront infuriated everyone and, in a moment, all officers without an exception moved towards him with such threatening gestures that I was convinced they would murder him on the spot. I interfered at once, moved them aside and got to Captain Bock to protect

---

[88] Pushin refers to Yegor Yegorovich Bock, who served as a staff captain in the Life Guard Semeyonovskii Regiment.

[89] Bock's fault was that he acted cowardly during battles. Thus, I. Yakushkin remembered that during the battle of Borodino one Russian officer "decided to pull a prank on Bock, who was a well known coward in the Semeyonovskii Regiment: he snuck upon him from behind and threw a fistful of dirt at him. Bock was so frightened that he fell to the ground." I. Yakushkin, *Zapiski, statii, pisma…*, 153.

him. After quieting officers, I demanded Captain Bock surrender his sword and told him that he was arrested for an outrageous behavior that he dared to commit by appearing at my gathering to cause a fight with officers whom he met 100 times a day in other places. I immediately sent him, escorted by my battalion adjutant, to *hautpwache* and then went in person to our General Potemkin to inform him about this incident and give him Bock's sword. I quickly realized that the general was protecting Bock but, I could not care less about him, I avoided getting into argument of accusing or justifying Bock, and simply remarked that I could not have acted differently both out of concerns for Bock's safety and respect for officer community. I then returned to Lavernua, where my officers awaited me. We got back to the table and their furor gradually subsided.[90]

13 [25] January. Tuesday.

Standing still. We received the order to take additional buildings for quartering so as to rest more comfortably.

14 [26] January. Wednesday.

In consequence of the order received the day before, I marched with my battalion to the commune of Chézeaux. I quartered at the house of a local cure, a kind and charitable old man. We stayed here for a couple of days.

16 [28] January. Friday

Bourbonne-les-Bains[91] is located about two miles from Chézeaux. Accompanied by several officers, I traveled there to spend a day. I cannot say anything about the curing powers of local waters but Bourbonne-les-Bains looks pitiful and we felt very uncomfortable there. This region has nothing to offer and the curé's village was a much better place so we returned there in the evening.

17 [29] January. Saturday.

---

[90] Bock was soon transferred as a major to the Aleksandriiskii Hussar Regiment.

[91] Bourbonne-les-Bains was known as a health resort due to its thermal springs that have been used since Roman times.

We finally left the vicinity of Langres where we have remained since the 10th. We marched in the direction of Chaumont for thirteen hours in an atrocious weather. My battalion occupied quarters at Boulangy [Poulangy]. The poverty in this region is staggering; people are deprived of most necessities while in Champagny they are dying of thirst. Our quarters are chilly and dirty...

18 [30] January. Sunday.

We passed through Chaumont, the administrative center of the Haute Marne, and occupied quarters at Laharmand. After letting my regiment pass, I stayed for a while at Chaumont but found nothing interesting there, this was a rather pitiful city.

19 [31] January. Monday.

We received order to bivouac at Colombey [-les-Deux-Eglises], but we had hardly deployed there when an order arrived for us to return to quarters. So we marched back for two miles to take up quarters at Meures not far from Laharmand. Would not it have been better if we were not moved at all?

20 January [1 February]. Tuesday.

Our corps departed at 6 am and proceeded towards Bar-sur-Aube. After passing through this town, we turned right and bivouacked around 8 p.m. Throughout this time there was a strong cannonade in the advance guard. The snow was coming down in large snowflakes and a strong wind was blowing.

21 January [2 February]. Wednesday.

The Battle at Brienne. Our corps broke its camp at 1 a.m. at night. It proceeded towards Brienne-le-Château to form the reserves of General [Fabian] [Osten-]Sacken, who had engaged the enemy in battle. The fighting began at 8 a.m. in the morning. We did not participate in it because even without our support the enemy was completely defeated by 4 p.m. Snow and wind made our condition completely unbearable. Fortunately, as soon as victory became certain, we were ordered to take quarters. We marched on the road leading to Troyes and stopped at the village of Mont-Martin.

22 January [3 February]. Thursday.

We hoped for a day break at Mont-Martin when, around noon, we suddenly received an order to march. [My servant] Luka returned from Frankfurt where he left [my mistress] Elizabeth Sperl and found me at my quarters just prior to our departure from Mont-Martin. We moved hoping to bivouac but soon received order to occupy quarters. We halted at Montieramey. We were not assigned quarters and therefore occupied them on our own discretion. I got a rather deplorable quarter. The host was father of nine small children and our arrival so frightened him that I had to use various means to calm him down. We were in the department of Aube, which is no better than Haute Marne.

23 January [4 February]. Friday.

Despite horrible bed which I found at the house, I slept like a dead men because of extreme exhaustion of the previous day. I woke up on at 6 a.m. since, under orders received the day before we had to march maintaining great order to Troyes. But the indecision, typical to our commanders, particularly after we entered France, showed its face once more. Another order arrived cancelling the first and we stayed at Montieramey. I decided to find new quarters where settled in a bit better conditions than in the first.

24 January [5 February]. Saturday.

We left Montieramey in the morning and proceeded to Bourguignons, where we crossed the Seine River over a very narrow bridge. Here we heard the sound of cannon fire and soon received the order to halt the entire corps. We then changed our direction and marched to Troyes, that is, to the sound of gunfire. The weather was nice, with some ten degrees of frost, which did not dispose us to staying at bivouacs. About half an hour after we moved in this new direction, we were ordered to turn back and had to move through Bar-sur-Seine to Polisy, where we took new quarters.

25 January [6 February]. Sunday.

We marched at 7 a.m. My battalion hardly reached Villiers-sous-Praslin as I received a new order to proceed with two companies to Praslin. There I occupied quarters with the Austrian troops. In the afternoon our entire regiment was ordered to move. It was raining heavily. We departed at 5 p.m. and, after marching for 3 miles (12 verstas) [8 miles], stopped at quarters at Vanlay around 10 p.m. I was wet to my bones and extremely annoyed by the meaningless exhaustion that we were subjected to since we, for all practical purposes, remained in the same place.

26 January [7 February]. Monday.

We were forced to march hastily through Chaffois to Ville-Morugne [?], where our entire corps was supposed to concentrate to participate in the attack on Troyes. However, because the French had abandoned this town, there was no fighting and so we marched, without stooping at Ville-Morugne, towards Chapitre, which is located not far from Villiers-sous-Praslin. Thus, if I were not forced to march yesterday morning, I would not even have to move today.

27 – 28 January [8-9 February]. Wednesday.

Standing still. Order is issued for everyone to wear a white arm-band on the left hand, that is, all the Allied troops had to wear it. People assure that this is to show that we are on the side of the Bourbons.

29 January [10 February]. Thursday.

We marched for 4 miles (16 verstas) [10 miles] to occupy quarters at Troyes, the administrative center of the Aube department. I settled in the Saint Martin suburb. The city struck me as large and well built but the circumstances, as well as large number of people concentrated there, prevented me from obtaining even most basic necessities. Besides, we were received very poorly here.

30 January [11 February]. Friday.

We were already under arms and ready to march when the order arrived for to us stay put. The Imperial headquarters was located in town so I took an opportunity to pay respects to Count Arakcheyev and then spent the entire day walking along the streets. We wondered so much around Troyes that we nicknamed this period of our campaign as the Troyens War.[92] In reality we could have occupied Troyes immediately after the battle at Brienne, but we outwitted ourselves and prolonged this pleasure for another ten days.

---

92 A play of words on the Trojan War.

31 January [12 February]. Saturday.

We marched at 6 a.m., remained on the road until 5 pm and halted at Maizières-la-Grande-Paroisse, where we took quarters. Here we learned that [the French] captured our entire division (Olsufiev's) with all of its generals and officers.

FEBRUARY

1 - 2 [13-14] February. Sunday and Monday.

Now we cannot even get enough sleep. We were woken up at 1 am at night and ordered to march to Mesgrigny, where we remained at bivouacs until 11 a.m. before we returned back to our quarters at Maizières-la-Grande-Paroisse. We found this village completely empty because all of its residents fled during our excursion into Mesgrigny. One can imagine what a disheartening impression the sight of abandoned homes had on us. We occupied them in spite of hardship we experienced in the absence of their owners and remained there until 6 pm when drums began to beat and we were ordered to leave. The weather was beautiful but the darkness fell rapidly, we were tired and sleepy and not predisposed to enjoying scenery. After passing through Nogent-sur-Seine, we stopped for a rest and, after an hour, moved again, marching all night long. Finally, around 5 a.m. on the 2nd [of February], Monday, we reached La Motte [-Tilly], where we took up quarters. I dropped on the bed and slept like a dead man until noon.

3 - 4 [15-16] February. Tuesday and Wednesday.

We remained at La Motte till 7 p.m. on Tuesday. We even began to hope that our superiors will let us have a peaceful rest but alas, suddenly an order was issued and all troops marched at once, moving through Nogent and made a rest at Romilly [-sur-Seine] when it was already dark; we soon feel asleep. This rest unexpectedly lasted until 8 a.m. on Wednesday, the 4th. A new order soon arrived which, instead of sending us to Arcis, instructed us to march once again to Nogent, where we had to take up quarters. At Nogent, I was fortunate to receive very nice quarters.

5 [17] February. Thursday.

I took pleasure in staying at my quarters all day long, counting on spending the night here as well. My dinner and bed were already prepared when suddenly, around 9 p.m., alarm was sounded. Farewell my hope for restful night. I had to bid good-bye to my warm room and march in rather nippy wind at night. Fortunately, we marched for only three quarters of a mile [0.7 km] and stopped near Le Grez [?].

6 [18] February. Friday.

Our entire corps moved at the same time as we did in the morning and bivouacked at Trainel.

7 [19] February. Saturday.

Our corps departed at 5 a.m. and still withdrawing along the road to Troyes, it bivouacked at Prunay[-Belleville].

8 [20] February. Sunday.

We departed at 3 a.m. at night, still in the same direction. Bivouacked at La Malmaison, about one mile [4.24 km] away from Troyes.

9 [21] February. Monday.

There are strong rumors that peace will be concluded.

10 [22] February. Tuesday.

Rumors keep changing every minute. Now nobody speaks of peace, instead we are told that hostilities resumed. Our corps departed at 5 a.m.; after reaching the suburbs of Troyes, it turned left and bivouacked at Saint-Parres-aux-Tertres, while I led my battalion to its quarters at Baires and served as an outpost.

11 – 12 [23-24] February. Wednesday and Thursday.

The Corps broke its camp around 6 p.m. on Wednesday. I joined it and, as marching together, we reached Lusigny [-sur-Barse] in awful darkness around 9 p.m. and bivouacked there. Fortunately I found right next to our bivouac a small hut where I spent the night since it was better to stay inside than under open sky. At 2 a.m. at night of 12 February we were ordered to march once more. The frost was quite strong. At 6 a.m.

we arrived at Vendeuvre [-sur-Barse] and bivouacked there. At 5 p.m. we marched again and reached Bar-sur-Aube by midnight.

In general, our situation is highly unpleasant. We march for entire days, arrive in places late at night and then wait for hours before bonfires are set so we can warm ourselves, all of which is rather strenuous in current cold.

13 [25] February. Friday.

Our corps left Bar-sur-Aube at 7 a.m. It marched for a second time into the Haute Marne department and, at 4 p.m., bivouacked at Colombey-les-Deux-Eglises, where it had already been on 19 January. We stayed here for about two hours. After marching once more, we halted about three quarters of a mile away [0.7 km] from Chaumont, where we spent the night.

14 [26] February. Saturday.

We marched from 9 a.m. till 11 p.m. today. This was of course rather exhausting but the knowledge that we will have quarters instead of bivouacs made us ignore our fatigue. We stopped two [Russian] miles [5 miles] from Langres in the commune of Courcelles-en-Montagne.[93]

15 [27] February. Sunday.

Day of rest.

16 [28] February. Monday.

Our regiment marched at 4 a.m. It was already approaching Chaumont where the order arrived to stop and take quarters at Brottes.

17 - 22 February [1-6 March]. Tuesday to Sunday.

Our Corps was ordered to occupy extensive quarters so we can settle down more comfortably. So my regiment marched about one and half mile [south] and occupied the village of Crenay. We stayed here until the 23td. This FIVE day respite, which we so badly needed, caused numerous outlandish rumors, one wilder than another. I do not even want to repeat them since I do not know where the rest of our army is located and find it

---

[93] By now, Pushin's men had marched some 200 km in nine days.

more prudent to wait for events to unfold instead of acting based on these rumors. I can only say that our forces are far greater to the enemy ones for us to be concerned of complications and that our situation is incomparably superior compared to 1812.

23 February [7 March]. Monday.

We departed at 9 a.m. and marched in countryside for about three miles [12.7 km] before taking quarters at Breaux [?].

28 February [12 March]. Saturday.

After five day respite, we marched at 6 a.m. We occupied the road leading from Chaumont to Troyes and then marched to Joinville, taking quarters at Leschères [-sur-le-Blaiseron], not far from that town.

MARCH

1 [13] March. Sunday.

At 9 a.m. we suddenly received an order to depart and, at 11 a.m., our regiment marched through Doulevant towards Mertrud, where it took quarters.

2 - 3 [14-15] March. Monday-Tuesday.

Alarm was sounded at 10 a.m. The regiment marched at once. We made an enormous march.[94] Passed through Montier [-en-Der] and, at 2 a.m. on Tuesday morning, arrived to our quarters at Vaucogne. We are back in the Aube department.

4 March [16]. Wednesday.

We had barely departed from Vaucogne when [troops] arrived to prepare quarters for the Lithuanians [Life Guard Litovskii Regiment]. Our regiment moved at 7:30 a.m. and, after marching for two mile [8.5 km], it took quarters at Aubigny. The corps was supposed to concentrate around Ramerupt. Around 6 p.m. we marched back for about 3 miles [12.7 km] and took quarters at Donnement, where we spent the night.

---

[94] Pushin's men must have marched at least 50 km that day.

5 March [17]. Thursday.

Our regiment left Donnement at 7 a.m., passed through Brienne-le-Château, where Napoleon grew up. Our corps gathered here as well and bivouacked at La Rothière.

6 March [18]. Friday.

The weather was so nice that staying in bivouacs was not as dire anymore, but we were soon marching again. The Corps departed before 8 a.m. We marched through Brienne once again and took quarters at Chalette [-sur-Voire], about two miles [8.5 km] from the town.

7 March [19]. Saturday.

The regiment departed at 4 a.m. to proceed to our corps' concentration point at Jevr [?]. We then marched [back] in the direction to Brienne and took positions at Perthes [lès-Brienne]. It was said that the enemy would attack us here.

8-9 [20-21] March. Sunday-Monday.

We left our positions at Perthes at 6 a.m. on Sunday morning, crossed the Aube River at Lesmont and proceeded towards the heights near Longsols. It was initially planned to bivouack here but since the battle at Arcis had began by then, we only made a short rest at Longsols and continued to march for the entire day before finally bivouacking at Voué. At 2 a.m. at night of 9 March our corps was placed under arms once again and dispatched in battle order by battalions towards Arcis-sur-Aube, where ti took up positions with its right flank anchored on the village of Chaudrey.

We were in the front line but, until around 4 p.m., nothing decisive was attempted either on our or enemy side. Light fighting between our and enemy skirmishers resembled more a fun game than a battle. The situation remained like this until all our forces arrived. Three gun salvos signaled the start of our attack. The French could not resist our charge and our troops entered Arcis without a difficulty; it was only then that we realized that we were facing a small enemy force. Our corps, joined by the Bavarians, marched towards Lesmont, crossed the Aube River and proceeded on the road to Chalons in order to cut the enemy line of retreat. We bivouacked about one mile [4.24 km] from Lesmont around 3 a.m. on Tuesday night.

10 [22] March. Tuesday.

At 2 p.m., our corps moved again, making a parade march in front of the commander-in-chief at Chalette and bivouacking at Dampiere.

11 [23] March. Wednesday.

We left our bivouacs at Dampiere before noon. At 3 p.m. we stopped at Soldesois and resumed march several hours later. We bivouacked again only as the night fell at Cheron [?]. For the past few days we marched under the sound of military music and victory songs. Today happiness revealed itself early on. We learned that two squadrons of the Guard uhlans captured 20 enemy cannon.[95] Cannonade could be heard throughout the day and we assumed that there will be a decisive battle tomorrow.

12 [24] March. Thursday.

Our corps marched at 5 a.m. and covered 3-4 miles [13-17 km] before bivouacking at Kole [?]. People assert that Napoleon and his main army have moved into our rear.

13 [25] March. Friday.

The infantry of our corps departed before 6 a.m. and rested at Poivres. We learned here that our cavalry, which was moving ahead of us, had engaged the enemy but we heard about the details and outcome of the battle only after reaching Connantray [-Vaurefroy]. The details were as follows:

The entire French army was numerically far inferior to our entire army which flooded Emperor Napoleon's realm. So Napoleon, in order to delay our march on Paris, decided to direct his main forces against line of operations, leaving only two corps under Marshal Marmont between us and his capital. Emperor Napoleon undoubtedly hoped that we, frightened by his daring maneuver, would immediately turn and march to the Rhine but events unfolded contrary to that. Napoleon was pursued

---

[95] Pushin refers to an incident at Sompuis where, on 23 March, the Guard uhlans attacked Marshal Macdonald's rear guard and captured 27 guns and 400 men.

only by a cavalry corps commanded by General Wintzingorode while the Allied monarchs, with the rest of their armies, went on offensive to destroy Marmont, who was defeated at Arcis and other places, and finally at La Fère Champenoise, loosing many prisoners and 30 guns.

14-15 [26-27] March. Saturday-Sunday.

At 6 a.m. on Saturday, our corps marched once again. We stopped at Sézanne and then kept marching until 2 a.m. on Sunday night, when we bivouacked at Le Vézier. At 8 a.m. we were on the move once more and after passing La Ferté-Gaucher we proceeded to Coulommiers, where we bivouacked only at 11 p.m.

16 [28] March. Monday.

We covered approximately 5 miles (20 verstas) [21.2 km] today. Our corps passed through Crécy[-la-Cha[elle] in the direction of Meaux, the departments of Seine and Marne, and bivouacked at Nanteuil[-lès-Meaux]. The views of the countryside we are passing in are very picturesque and I assume the local residents probably enjoyed prosperity that is [now] destroyed by the current war.

17 [29] March. Tuesday.

We crossed the Marne River at Meaux, a rather beautiful town. Our corps then proceeded through Claye to its bivouacs at Villeparisis. We are finally at the walls of Paris, and eagerly awaited the dawn of the decisive tomorrow day! Moscow will be avenged at last. A few proclamations already appeared revealing the rising great danger for Napoleon.

18 [30] March. Wednesday.

The Battle at Montmartre. Our corps marched at 7 a.m. in the direction of Belleville, which was already attacked by the 3rd Corps. The battle began almost simultaneously with our departure. The French fought courageously at Belleville but were forced to submit to our superior numbers and our corps, except for the Prussians, whose Guard remained in the reserves and, despite fighting like lions at Panten [?], its troops took no part in today's battle since the 3rd Corps, which we were reinforcing, did not waiver even for a minute in its confidence of victory and required no assistance. Belleville was captured; our center, that is the position between Belleville and Montmartre, also operated successfully. The

Emperor [Alexander] and King of Prussia, as well as the entire General Staff soon arrived and took position on the Belleville heights from where they had a clear view of the entire battlefield. We all were extremely nervous, our hearts were pounding as the moment of the surrender of Paris approached; [meantime] General [Osten-]Sacken with his corps was still one day's march behind us in order to oppose Napoleon who, having heard about our offensive on Paris, moved by forced marches to attack us from the rear. [Everyone] was concerned that he would arrive before the [French] capital was in our hands, which would have produced God knows what kind of results. During the day the Emperor [Alexander] received several negotiators and at the moment when it seemed that he was losing patience with all these negotiations, an adjutant arrived with a report that Count Langeron's corps had occupied the heights of Montmartre. Indeed, shortly before 4 p.m., we saw Count Langeron's advance guard, under command of [Lieutenant-]General [Alexander] Rudzevich, deploying in attack columns, taking by assault Montmartre, which was the last position still defended by the French. We saw how the French fled and sent their messenger with an offer of surrender. The Emperor, gleaming with happiness, mounted his horse and congratulated us with the capture of Paris. A thundering 'hurrah' spread along our ranks. We marched by Their Majesties [Alexander and King Frederick William III], passed Belleville, and bivouacked [in the field] with our left wing anchored on Belleville. Many Parisian women visited our camps that evening.

19 [31] March. [Thursday]. Triumphant Entry into Paris

Excitement prevented us from sleeping; we were ready [for march] much earlier than we were required. Our columns were deployed long before the Emperor arrived to lead the troops. We entered the city [of Paris] exactly at noon. We marched in the following order: [Our] sovereign's flugel-adjutants; [Our] Sovereign, King of Prussia, princes, field marshals, commander-in-chief and others; 3rd Army Corps; Austrian grenadiers; 2nd Russian Guard Division; Prussian Guard Infantry; 1st Guard Division and all of cavalry; [followed by] artillery.

We entered through Fauburg Saint Martin. Crowds of onlookers increased as we advanced into the city and all of them expressed genuine happiness, shouting "Vive Alexander! Vive King of Prussia! Vive Bourbons!" But can we really believe in any of this? Just yesterday these same people were yelling "Vive Napoleon." Reaching the boulevards, we marched along them to Grand Meuble and then crossed the Place de la Revolution to enter the Champs-Elysèes. Here the monarchs stopped and, as [Parisians] mobbed them, we marched in front of Their Majesties.

The Parisians were truly stunned by this spectacle. They were assured that only a small blundering column of our troops was marching on Paris, but now they saw a powerful army of splendid appearance in front of them. Passing by Their Majesties, our regiment halted in the Widow Alley, where we remained till 8 p.m. The regiment was then sent to barracks to spend the night. The Preobrazhenskii Regiment was assigned to guard the Emperor, who settled in the Hotel de Talleyrand; one battalion of the Preobrazhenskii Regiment surrounded the Hotel while two others occupied the Champs-Elysées.

Meantime, we, drunk with happiness, found a meager tavern owner not far from our barracks and he delivered to us a rather paltry dinner, which we, nevertheless, immediately devoured as a consequence of an arduous day.

20 March [1 April]. Friday.

[Today], our regiment guarded the Emperor. It was deployed in battle formation on the Place de la Revolution and our music [band] played as we waited for the arrival of His Majesty. The famous hymn of Henry IV[96] made a profound impression on numerous onlookers who, as expected, gathered around us. Many of them already wear white bands on their left hands as do we. As both monarchs [Alexander and Frederick William] appeared in front of our ranks, the crowd's excitement increased and the same shouts, as the day before, began to be heard again. We made a parade march, the 1st Battalion then proceeded to the Hotel de Talleyrand while two other battalions remained on the Champs-Elysées; the third battalion bivouacked on the right side while the second on the left. This time we had a glorious dinner and, unwilling to risk moving to far from our positions, we were unable to explore streets. In the evening, however, I still managed to walk a bit in the Palais Royal.

21 March [2 April]. Saturday.

Our regiment woke up early in the morning. Officers received billets in the city, the soldiers were moved into Imperial barracks on the Quai Malaquar. I was given an apartment of M. Bourdeau on the Rue Croix de

---

[96] Pushin refers to Marche Henri IV or Vive Henri IV which served as the nominal anthem of the Bourbon dynasty during the Ancient Regime. During the Revolutionary and Napoleonic Era, the song became a rallying cry for the royalists.

Petit Champs. Taking advantage of this first free day, I immediately went to see the Hotel des Invalides. I visited the new bridge, Arc de Triomphe separating the Tuileries Palace on the Place du Carrousel and the Notre Dame Cathedral. The Provisional government announced the toppling of Napoleon and declared his subjects to be [under the authority of] the Bourbons from now on.

22 March [3 April]. Sunday.

Today I went to see the Pantheon, which Napoleon did not complete yet. Still, under its arches, one can already see the tombs of Voltaire, Rousseau and other great men of France. The New Pantheon is located very close from Saint-Geneviève, the most ancient church in Paris, built during the reign of King Clovis I. I then went to the Botanical Garden [*Jardin des Plantes*], where I saw a zoo that contains virtually all species of known animals. I was unable to get into a zoological cabinet because it is usually open only three times a week.

Leaving Botanical Garden, I crossed the Pont d'Austerlitz and, following the boulevards, I walked throughout the city. This long stroll did not tire me at all. [Later in the day] I even walked for a bit more in the garden of the Tuileries Palace, where numerous people congregated. I returned home around 6 p.m. and dined with my hosts, whose carefulness towards me I cannot praise enough. The family consisted of old mother Madam Bourdeau, who occupied the second floor and rarely came down, M. Berten, his wife and their sons Alexis, Henri and daughter Adelie, and finally M. Berten's brother, Alexander Berten, who spent considerable time in emigration in Germany.

After the dinner I left the dining room to go to the Theatre Francais. Both comedies were perfectly played. The Emperor attended the play and, expressing his approval of actors, he compelled the public to applaud, for which Paris is rather susceptible. Particularly thundery and widespread applause began during entr'acte when the lowered stage curtain revealed an ancient French coat of arms, the fleurs-de-lis painted on a sheet of paper. The shouts "Vive Alexander, our savior! Vive le Roi" could be heard from every direction and hats with white cockades quickly became vogue. The Senate, the guardian of laws, officially declared that it no longer acknowledges Napoleon [as a ruler of France.]

23 March [4 April]. Monday.

I went to see the Louvre and the Museum. Both owe so much to Napoleon. Architecture of the Louvre will forever serve as a monument for this unordinary man. The works of art gathered here from all countries of Europe during last few years represent everything that is breathtaking in this world. I saw here the statues of Apollo Belvedere, Venus de Milo, Laocoon, Raphael's *Resurrection of Christ* and many others. I took pleasure in the newest works of art and would have happily spent entire day in looking at all of these marvels if only several of my friends had not distracted me from my diversion and dragged me to the Palais Royal, a more simply and marvelous place, and no less interesting as well. In the evening I went to the *Theatre des Varietes* and must acknowledge that Brenot's [?] sharp wit brought me great pleasure.

Napoleon, and the remnants of his army, arrived at Fontainebleau. Despite all the advantages of our situation, he still instilled some concern and we were ordered to prepare for battle.

24 March [5 April]. Tuesday.

French marshals Ney, Macdonald, Mortier and Marmont, as well as Caulaincourt, visited the Emperor today and informed him that Napoleon agreed to abdicate his throne but only in favor of his son.

26 March [7 April]. Thursday.

Today I was at the Longchamp [Abbey] but it is unimpressive. Maybe it is because of turbulent times.[97] The famous festival here usually starts on Wednesday after the Easter and continues for three days.

29 March [10 April]. Easter Sunday.

A large mass was held on the Place de la Concord, also known as Place de la Revolution. The entire Guard was under arms, made a parade march in front of the Emperor and then deployed in closed battalion columns around prie-dieu[98] erected at the very spot where the French once beheaded the unfortunate Louis XVI. Now this same spot saw prayers reaching to the heavens to thank the Lord for a fortune turn of events that led to the accession of Louis XVIII on the French throne. Napoleon's marshals were present as well and had to kneel when [the accession] was announced under the thunder of Russian guns.

---

[97] The Longchamp Abbey was almost completely destroyed during the French Revolution.

[98] Pushin uses a Russian term "analoi" to refer to prie-dieu which was a special type of prayer desk.

31 March [12 April]. Tuesday.

Count d'Artois[99] made his entry into Paris. Large crowds greeted him, indescribable joy. After escorting Madam Berten to the boulevards, I could stay with her to wait for the prince's arrival because I had to dine with all colonels of the Russian and Prussian guards at the Emperor's place. At 6 p.m. Count d'Artois, who was declared as lieutenant du Roi, appeared in front of the Emperor [Alexander]. Napoleon's abdication, signed by him the day before at Fontainebleau,[100] was publicly announced today.

APRIL

1 [13] April. Wednesday.

M. Berten owned an estate at Rueil where he invited me to visit them. We covered the tree mile long trip between breakfast and lunch. Also near Rueil there is a small Chateau de Malmaison, the last refuge of Empress Josephine. Although this place is not spacious enough for an empress, it is, nevertheless, very beautiful, particularly a small statue, famous for its antiquity, which Napoleon brought with him from Egypt. Some people assure that it is over 4,000 years old. After lunch, for which I was invited by my hosts in Paris, I traveled to the Luxembourg Garden but because the garden is usually open until 7 p.m., I was not able to get inside and instead enjoyed the exquisite architecture of Saint Sulpice Church and then returned home crossing the Pont des Arts.

2 [14] April. Thursday.

Yearning to visit the Lixembrourg Palace at any cost, I went there immediately after breakfast. It was wonderful but was visited by fewer people than the Tulleries Garden. I did not enter the palace. Returning home, I entered Saint Sulpice Church. This enormous building is decorated with marvelous columns and very beautiful murals.

3 [15] April. Friday.

---

[99] Charles, Count d'Artois, was the brother of Louis XVI and Louis XVIII, and the future king of France.

[100] Napoleon signed unconditional abdication on 11 April.

The Austrian emperor made a celebratory entry into Paris today. On this account, we all were placed under arms, and showed no particular excitement about it. During the entire French campaign the Austrians contributed very little to our successes. As we entered France, a large number of the Austrian troops and Emperor Francis himself proceeded to Lyons, where they had no combats with the enemy. Still, the French admonished the Austrian emperor that he contributed to the misfortune of his own son-in-law.

[…]

9 [21] April. Thursday.

Duc de Berry, the son of Count d'Artois and nephew of the king, entered Paris today. He was greeted quite cheerfully and, when he entered the Tuilleries, the crowd rushed inside the garden demanding that the prince appear on a balcony. He finally appeared with his father, who kissed him lovingly which caused general excitement and applause. My attention was drawn to an old lady, who kept grabbing my hand with tears streaming from her eyes and continually yelling, "These caring princes, these precious princes." I later learned that this was a certain Madam Auverne, who once was a court lady but lost everything during the revolution; she came here with the crown to praise the princes whom she knew quite well and who have returned to their ancestors' palace as a result of extraordinary events.

11 [23] April. Saturday.

After lunch I went to see the former Augustine monastery, which is now a warehouse of various remarkable items gathered after the Revolution. The monastery is divided into the halls of the 13th, 14th, 15th and 16th centuries, and each hall is decorated in the style of that century. The halls of the 16th and 17th centuries have red glassworks, which are very beautiful. They largely show various stories, for example the story of Eros and Psyche, etc. There is no other place where you can observe the successive development of arts over five hundred years. Furthermore, each hall contains monuments to famous people of that century. The gardens also feature several monuments as well as the tombs of Abelard and Heloise, Molière, [Nicolas] Boileau [Despréaux] and others.

Leaving Saint Augustine, I went to Nortre Dame [Cathedral] where I climbed one of the towers to enjoy the panorama of Paris. Despite the tower's height, the city's narrow streets and tall building still did not allow me to observe these interesting environs and instead had to satisfy myself with a view of piled-up stones. I then went again to the Luxembourg Garden but this time I got inside the castle and was able to see its art gallery. One can finds the views of all port towns of France here.

12 [24] April. Sunday.

I finally received letters from Madam B. After the parade I went for a mass at the Saint Sulpice and, since I tried looking on Paris from above, I decided to climb one of the towers of this church as well. Although this tower is higher than that of Notre Dame, the panorama was even less interesting. The same sight of stacked stones, and you cannot even see the Seine River and its harbors from here.

In the evening, as usual, I went to theater. Today I was at Vaudeville. The last of three plays – "Tyrant Women" [by Blansini] was highly inappropriate and caused the public's outrage. People whistled fervently, while the play's author, enraged by such reception, insulted one of whistlers which led to a dreadful scandal which subsided only after the author was arrested. Such incidents are common occurrences in Parisian theaters.

15 [27] April. Wednesday.

We were introduced to Grand Dukes Nicholai [future Emperor Nicholas I] and Mikhail, who had recently arrived at Paris. They have grown up a lot.

19 April [1 May]. Sunday.

On the occasion of the restoration of the Bourbon dynasty, all theaters offer free passes today so one can imagine enormous crowds that besieged theater entrances since 1 p.m. Since decent people could not get inside theater, I took advantage of free time to walk with Madam Berten and her family along boulevards. We first went to the boulevard du Temple, visiting the Turkish Garden and the Princes' Garden.[101] They were bursting with people, illuminated and allowed bystanders to watch dancing artistes on ropes.

20 April [2 May]. Monday.

---

[101] The Jardin Turc and Jardin des Princes were famous and very popular café and gardens in the Marais district of Paris.

The French King Louis XVIII made a jubilant entry into Paris. There were enormous crowds of people. I was with Madam Berten and other ladies in a house near Pont Neuf and observed the procession. The town was illuminated in the evening. The Tuilleries Garden was magnificently illuminated but the fireworks, displayed on the Pont de Revolution, was rather meager.

22 April [4 May]. Wednesday.

We held a review after which we marched in a parade formation in front of the king. He can no longer sit on a horse so he was standing in one of the palace windows.

23 April [5 May]. Thursday.

Both the Bertens and their uncle Alexander offered me to travel to St. Cloud after lunch. We took one of those carriages, known as a coucou, that always stand near the Tuilleries. They harness one horse, are on two wheels and you have to sit in front. Four people easily fit inside but usually more people sit in them. So, traveling in such carriage we covered the sole mile that separates Paris from St. Cloud. Unfortunately we arrived too late to see everything that was interesting since dusk was expected soon. But while Alexander and Alexis Bertens went to see horse which they wanted to buy, I and Henri Berten took a stroll in a park. The landscape is marvelous here but the chateau is quite small. I heard that it is magnificently decorated inside. The entire village, located on a hill on the Seine riverbank, represents an enthralling sight. The same can be said about everything found on the road from Paris to St. Cloud. The road runs through the Bois de Boulogne, the village of the same name and streaks along the Seine River. We returned to Paris at 10 p.m. We were thoroughly searched at the gates to ensure that we are not transporting contraband. The contraband is handled rather strictly here and people are not allowed to transport even two bottles of wine inside Paris without paying a fee for them.

27 April [9 May]. Monday.

During breakfast M. Berten (father) got an idea to travel to Versailles. I naturally eagerly agreed to accompany and so the three of us – M. Berten, M. Portier and me, went. M. Portier, a jovial merry fellow, made us laugh the entire trip. We could not stop to see the famous porcelain factory at Sevres since we were hurrying to Versailles, where we, despite all our haste, arrived only at 3 p.m. Versailles is a very beautiful town. The façade of the palace, facing the road from Paris, is very handsome, and stables built in semi-circle greatly adorn it. As soon as we stopped, a certain person, very courteous, appeared and offered to show us everything noteworthy in Versailles. We accepted his offer and here is what I deduced from the Versailles sight-seeing.

The library, beside books that embellish it, contains several idols brought from the Americas, models of various vessels, a skeleton of a small creature which closely resembles a human one, except for its skull. The Versailles Park has seven miles (about 28 verstas) in its circumference and is magnificent, although it is monotonously planned. The palace façade from the park is fabulous and was refurbished by Napoleon. Thus edifice, built by Louis XIV, is enormous and its opulence cannot be compared to anything else. Here even the superb bronze and marble statues by great masters seem rather casual and ordinary creations.

The palace itself is located on a hill, whose slope descends into a garden with numerous fountains which, however, cannot operate during entire day but only a few hours because the famous mechanism,[102] which supplies water from Marly two miles away, cannot provide enough water to operate all fountains for entire day. I came to conclusion that our Peterhof garden[103] is incomparably better. The Grand and Petit Trianon are two small palaces inside the Versailles park. Their architecture and interior are scrupulously maintained. Napoleon lived in the former at one time. The art gallery and malachite vases were given by Emperor Alexander as gifts to the French emperor when they were still in good relations. The interior of the main Versailles palace has been neglected since the years of the Revolution. Gilded decorations attracted attention as remnants of opulence which once adorned this palace. Nevertheless, the palace theater and church are still in good conditions and deserve attention.

After completing sight-seeing we went to eat at a tavern and since M. Berten had several acquaintances in Versailles, we visited them before returning to Paris at 10 p.m. If I ever have a chance, I will certainly return to Versailles to see it more casually and not as hurriedly as we did it today.

---

[102] Pushin refers to the famous Machine de Marly, a French engineering marvel built by Arnold de Ville and Rennequin Sualem in 1684 to supply water to the Versailles Palace and its fountains. The machine consisted of consisted of fourteen gigantic water wheels, each about thirty-six feet wide, that moved dozens of pumps to bring water up a hillside from the Seine River.

[103] Pushin refers to the Peterhof Palace founded by Peter the Great and completed by Empress Elizabeth in mid-18th century.

MAY

7 [19] May. Thursday.

Twice a week, a festivity is held in Tivoli Gardens[104] situated on the outskirts of Paris. Usually, these festivals are held on Thursdays and Sundays. Today the fête was declared an exceptional, so how could I miss it? Shortly before 8 pm, I took a carriage and went to Tivoli. Going through a long, lighted alley I came to the entrance. Here people were asked to leave their canes, swords, etc. so I did as requested, bought a ticket, which, because of exceptional nature of this particular festivity, was worth 5 francs, when it usually costs 3 francs. The whole garden was illuminated and full of people. The first thing that struck me was this round grove which contained, both on the left and right, cosmoramas (illuminated pictured). They depicted the sights of Italy: on one side - a volcanic eruption, on the other - a valley. A very pleasant music calmed our mood. Further on, mothers entertained their children with puppets, which also drew attention of adults because they were indeed very entertaining. Moving on, I heard pleasant voices singing to the accompaniment of two violins and two harps so I stopped to listen to them. When this little concert was over, I continued my way but soon heard the sound of quadrille,[105] performed by a large orchestra, so I stopped to watch the pretty dancers. A few steps away – swings, shooting galleries, and thousands of other entertainments that all caught my attention. Finally, two juggler in different places completely befuddled me and I did not know where to go and what to see first. In conclusion, this beautifully illuminated garden presented a magnificent sight and I did not notice how time passed before 9 o'clock. Artists on a tightrope also captivated my attention. After 10 pm magnificent fireworks were on display. I walked around until midnight, and I confess that 5 francs is a very small fee compared to the pleasure that one gains at this outdoor celebration in Tivoli.

11 [23] May. Monday.

Finding no place in the theater "Variety", I went to Mr. Pierre's *Cabinet mécanique*. This place is the height of perfection: it showed the island of

---

[104] Jardin de Tivoli, Paris, a garden and park open between 1766 and 1842, created to resemble the gardens of the Villa d'Este in Tivoli, Italy.

[105] Quadrille is an historic dance performed by four couples in a square formation, a precursor to traditional square dancing.

Corfu, with its ports and vessels sailing in and out; the Windsor Castle, traffic on the Thames, the movement of vehicles and pedestrians; valley of Montmorency, the famous place of residence J.-J. Rousseau; the port of Brest; a storm, etc. The whole mechanism is so simple that if not for the small dimensions that highlighted the lack of living people, one could just fall into error [of believing it was real.]

14 [26] May. Thursday.

Today, at 4 pm, I witnessed a very grizzly scene – the execution of counterfeiter performed at the Place de Grève. Usually, the guillotine is set up for a few hours before the execution and removed immediately after it is performed. The unfortunate was brought in by a gendarme in a cart. He did not mount the scaffold but was instead carried upon in because he was unconscious.

19 [31] May. Tuesday.

I wanted to visit Bagatelle, an English garden in the Bois de Boulogne, but the Duc de Berry, who visits it almost daily, has prohibited letting anyone in except on Mondays and Fridays; besides, a ticket was required to get in. So I, being on horseback, travelled along its wall and looked into the garden over the wall, unable to enter inside. However, from what I had seen I found Bagatelle to be a mere trifle, which I did not hope to see because a daily order announced our impending departure on Friday.

21 May [2 June]. Thursday.

Emperor Alexander has left Paris.

22 May [3 June]. Friday.

We left Paris in pouring rain at 9 am. King of Prussia was present at our departure. The corps headquarters went to St. Germain, while my battalion halted at Noisy, a few miles from St. Germain, at 6 pm. We passed through Marly and saw the famous [water wheel] machine [delivering water to Versailles] that seemed rather worn out which is hardly surprising since it survives since the time of Louis XIV. My host at Noisy is not particularly polite, but his house, and the garden in particular, is very beautiful.

23 May [4 June]. Saturday.

Today, I went to spend the day in Paris. I had to travel 6 verstas, passing through Saint-Cloud. You cannot describe the joy of the Bertin family when I arrived. I could not refuse their lunch and I spent the rest of the time on shopping until it was time to go to the theater. I was at Fabo, and since it was too late to return to Noisy, I stayed the night in Paris and asked permission to spend the night at Mademoiselle Louise Chatelet, Rue Valois, she was my kept woman, so I was accepted with open arms and spent a fun time.

24 May [5 June]. Sunday.

I left Paris this morning. A carriage took me to Versailles for 40 centimes. Here I had a lunch with such an appetite that one can develop after travelling for four verstas. I was still a half mile from Noisy, which proved to be difficult to travel since I had to hire a carriage specifically for this trip. This pleasure cost me 6 francs. I reached Noisy at 3 pm. Here I found a large gathering at my host' house; among them were Parisians who tend to travel to nearby villages on Sundays. Dinner proved to be very lively, people sang witty ditties, which I really liked. In general, I was very pleased how I spent this day.

26 May [7 June]. Tuesday.

I left Noisy at 8 o'clock in the morning. The corps headquarters went to Mantes[-la-Jolie], and my battalion, after marching for seven verstas, stopped at La Bros. Location is very beautiful, but population is very poor. Mantes is located in the districts of the Seine and Oise.

27 May [8 June]. Wednesday.

Our regiment got to Mantaes, and after bivouacking at Bonnières, it reached Evreux at 8:30. The owner of the house, which housed the post office and where we stopped for breakfast, declined our money for the food we have ordered. Russians are particularly well respected in this area. Our march today was 11 verstas long.

28 May [9 June]. Thursday.

A day of rest at Evreux. There is nothing outstanding in this city. It does have a meager theater, which, after the Parisian ones, seemed to us even worse than it really was.

29 May [10 June]. Friday.

The regiment departed at 6 am, but I stayed for some time at Evreux, and caught up with the regiment only when it halted to rest. The march was again rather long. The regimental headquarters stopped at Bernay, my battalion passed this town and took quarters at the virtuous Saint Augustine. The area we traversed today is sparsely populated. A few villages are scattered here and there. Local residents, who hate the Bonapartes, gathered from afar to the main road where we were marching and expressed their particular delight on seeing us. People settle here quite differently than in the rest of France. Their dwellings are scattered in the forests, arable fields are located in between the ploughmen's houses. There are no vineyards at all but the local do make plenty of cider (apple wine). The owner of the house, where I was billeted, met me about one miles from the house. He frankly told me that he is very upset that I was going to spend only one night with him and that he desired for me to stay for at least 15 days. "These are our saviors," he told everyone [in the village].

30 May [11 June]. Saturday.

Our regiment marched out by companies. I stayed in St. Augustine until 10 am, then rode on a horse in the direction of Lisieux, where my battalion took up quarters in the suburbs. We are now in the district of Calvados.

31 May [12 June]. Sunday.

The divisional headquarters went to Argences, my battalion departed at 6 o'clock in the morning and stopped not far from this town, at a place called Magny-le-Freule. The reception extended to me by the local village head, who happened to be the owner of the house where I was billeted, surpassed all of my expectations. I knew that we were liked in Normandy, but I was in no way prepared when the mayor, accompanied by numerous people, came out in person to greet me with a white flag in hand and shouting: "Long live Alexander, our liberator," and so forth. Entering the village from the opposite side I somewhat disrupted their plans but despite this, M. de La Riviere (as the village head was called) was very attentive to me. He overwhelmed me with compliments, always ran to his cellar for the finest wines, treated me to all sorts of dishes, constantly repeating that I was now the master of the house and could I dispose of it as I wished it. His disproportionate courtesy became a nuisance. Excessiveness is a fault in everything.

JUNE

1 [13] June. Monday.

Our division moved to the village of Cagny and, after resting a bit, it entered Caen, the administrative center of Calvados. This city is quite populous and the suburb, where I was lodged, was beautiful. The street is sufficiently wide and features a few very attractive buildings.

2 [14] June. Tuesday.

A day of rest in Caen. This is a fairly large city; there are few public places and a place for festivities, called "short" - le court; this name is quite appropriate since the alley is very short, but very beautiful. Quay Orne also deserves some attention. The tomb of William the Conqueror is located in Caen.

3 [15] June. Wednesday.

Departing at 3 o'clock, we took up quarters at Bayeux. My [local] host served in Russia during the emigration year and spoke Russian. I greatly enjoyed talking to him about our country.

4 [16] June. Thursday.

The regiment departed at the same time as yesterday, that is, 3 o'clock at night, but I was too lazy to get up and slept until 5:00 am before catching up with the regiment. At 2 pm we stopped at Saint-Lo, the administrative center of the district of La Manche.

5 [17] June. Friday.

We again marched out at 3 am. The divisional headquarters went to Carentan, and my battalion to Beuzeville.

6 [18] June. Saturday.

A day of rest.

7 [19] June. Sunday.

The regiment departed by companies at 3 am, but I had the opportunity to sleep until 6 am and then traveled alone. The divisional headquarters moved to Valognes while my battalion proceeded to Montebourg.

8 [20] June. Monday.

The regiment departed at 4 o'clock in the morning. The division concentrated about half a mile from Cherbourg, and then triumphantly entered into the city. I then went with my battalion to Tour-la-Ville, where we received our lodgings.

9 [21] June. Tuesday.

I went to Cherbourg not so much out of curiosity but to take care of our business since we we are supposed to be loading onto ships in a few days. Since I had not right to an apartment [in the city] because I was assigned one in the village, I had to rent a room in a hotel, where I had all my belongings moved from the Tour-la-Ville. Then I began selling my horses, which we are not allowed to take with us onboard. I settled this business the way I wanted it.

10 [22] June. Wednesday.

Our second brigade, consisting of the [Life Guard] Ismailovskii and Jager Regiments, already boarded the ships and, taking advantage of favorable wind, it weighed anchor and sailed out. I spent the day exploring Cherbourg's famous harbor where human skill has accomplished more than nature. Napoleon undertook here works that are worthy of his greatness.

11 [23] June. Thursday.

My battalion moved to the city, where I got an apartment from one of my countrymen – an Estonian from Revel, who received me very cordially.

12 [24] June. Friday.

I received an order to load three companies of my battalion aboard the ship *Chesme*.[106] I wanted to first get acquainted with the sailors of the ship, so I went to dine with them on the ship. Even though the sea was calm, I did not feel well throughout my visit and could not eat well, so [returning to the city] I dined second time with my host.

13 [25] June. Saturday.

After a solemn prayer we all boarded the ships. Both Russian and French boats were used to transport out troops to the ships. I travelled with a part of my battalion in a French boat while the rest of the battalion boarded earlier. *Chesme* is a ship-of-the-line. I boarded it with the 4th, 5th and 6th companies of my battalion, while the 2nd Grenadier Company was placed on board of [another ship-of-the-line] *Jupiter* where our General Potemkin was as well. Chesme was commanded by Captain (2nd rank) [Dmitri] Shishmarev, but Rear Admiral [Ivan] Treskin [who commanded the entire naval squadron] was also present here.

14 [26] June. Sunday.

We weighed anchor at 8 o'clock in the morning. Upon leaving the raid, Admiral [Treskin], who commanded the squadron, gave the signal to line up in sailing order by two columns, each consisting of four battleships, except for a few smaller vessels that made up a third column. We then took course to NE in order to sail through the Channel, Pas de Calais and proceed to Deal. The rocking motion of the ship was negligible, but I was feeling dizzy nevertheless.

15 [27] June. Monday.

In the morning the wind was favorable, but then turned in opposite direction and finally completely disappeared. So at 8 pm we were forced to drop anchor.

16 [28] June. Tuesday.

---

[106] the 4th, 5th and 6th companies boarded *Chesme*. The 1st, 2nd and 3rd companies were on board of *Tri svyatitelya*, the 7th, 8th and 9th companies – on *Pamyat' Evstafiya*, while the regimental headquarters, three grenadier companies, musicians and non-combatants were placed on the ship *Jupiter*.

At 4 o'clock in the morning we set sail again and moved very slowly, but still saw the coast of England. By 9 o'clock the wind died down once more so we dropped anchor.

17 [29] June . Wednesday.

We set sail at 4 am and passed Dover at a very close range. At 2 pm still weather and opposite currents compelled us to drop anchor. We stood until 5 pm before a fair wind began to blow. We set sail and, at 7 pm, dropped anchor at Deal. The Admiral did not allow communicating with the shore, so despite our desire to visit the coastline, we were unable to do it today and went to sleep.

18 [30] June. Thursday.

Finally, the Admiral relented and allowed us to get ashore. Not wasting any time, I, with some of my officers, immediately boarded the boat. Sometimes the westerly wind greatly complicates landing at Deal; the shore is sloping so one must be very careful when approaching it. This time this inconvenience did not bother us but our desire to see the first English town was so great that no waves would have made us change our intentions. We finally landed, and I felt a peculiar pleasure in feeling a firm ground under my feet, even though it was the English soil.

Deal is a small town, very elegantly laid out. Houses and streets are kept very clean. Local merchandise is less elegant than the one of the neighboring places, and may be more durable, but they cost exorbitant money, even when compared with the prices in Paris. We went to dine at the tavern "Three Kings" where an ordinary lunch cost us 1 pound sterling each. The hospitals, judging from outward appearances because I did not look inside, are elegantly constructed and cleanly maintained. We returned to "Chesme" to spend the night.

19 June [1 July]. Friday.

Due to the high wind I could not go ashore until after noon. In the remaining short time I managed to make only a few purchases.

20 June [2 July]. Saturday.

At 3 pm, I again went ashore to stroll a little through the streets of Deal until 8 pm. By this time, we usually returned to the ship. Not knowing a word in English, I could not see much, which was frustrating but I was most impressed by our sailors. While we could not get locals to understand anything of what we were saying, our sailors had not a slightest difficulty with the English and got everything they wanted. [They would say] one or two words in English, then a strong expletive, a few gestures, and they were [perfectly] understood.

21 June [3 July]. Sunday.

On Sundays, everything seemingly dies out in England, shops are closed, people go to churches and then almost everyone sits at home. It was not even worth going ashore so we stayed on the ship. We held a church service aboard *Chesme* in the presence of the entire crew.

22 June [4 July]. Monday.

Despite relatively heavy sea, I went ashore to Deal at 9:00 am. I hired a carriage for the entire day for 18 shillings (about 18 rubles in our money), and, accompanied by [Gennadii] Kaznakov [a fellow officer from the LG Semeyonovskii Regiment], I went to Dover, which is about 9 English miles (1 English mile is - 1 3/4 versta) from Deal. At the barrier at Deal, we were asked to show the crew's pass and forced to pay 3 pence (1/4 shillings) for the right of way.

At 12 o'clock, we arrived at Dover. This city seemed to me a little larger than Deal. It has a pretty nice view, houses are not plastered, and the streets are very clean. To the left of the road on which we drove, on a hill near the sea, there was a castle that was built, according to the locals, by the Romans some ten centuries ago. At the foot of this particular hill, one can enjoy a very nice view of Dover. We were recommended an inn at Dover, and were even given its address, but we found it very difficult to find. Suddenly, an officer introduced himself to us and suggested to escort us there. This gentleman spoke French, which at first attracted us to him, but when we closely listened to his French which was as clear to us as was the English, we realized that our "cicerone"[107] is, in fact, an insufferable boor, so we tried our best to get rid of him, but could not do it for the rest of the day and he followed us like a shadow. The first thing we did was to have a breakfast and then went to see the castle. We enjoyed a beautiful view, and the port of Calais itself was clearly visible. Not being English and having a wretched interpreter, we were able to acquire only the most superficial information about this place. The antiquity of the

---

[107] Cicerone is a term for a guide one who conducts visitors and sightseers to museums, galleries, etc., and explains matters of archaeological, antiquarian, historic or artistic interest.

castle is easy to ascertain, its catacombs are very extensive. In one of the towers we were shown the grave of Julius Caesar himself, very simple, but incredibly large. Back in town, we went around the shops, which are few in number and are very poorly furnished so do not excite any desire to spend money. By 7 o'clock in the evening we returned to Deal, where we dined and went back to the ship. During today's travel I experienced the greatest pleasure while travelling from Deal to Dover. Charming location, wonderful field cultivation, and extraordinary cleanliness in villages. Looking at the surrounding orderliness you feel yourself as if in a garden. I must add that here, in England, I have not met a single beggar, although people say they are [plenty] of them in big cities.

23 June [5 July]. Tuesday.

In the afternoon, I went ashore for the last time and remained in Deal until 9 pm, buying all sorts of things before returning to the ship.

24 June [6 July]. Wednesday.

We set sail at 10 o'clock in the morning with a rather fresh tailwind. At 3 pm the coastline disappeared. The sea heaving was quite strong.

25 June [7 July]. Thursday.

The same wind direction, but the wind is much stronger than before. We sailed very quickly and, by 12 pm, it was calculated that we were 112 knots from Deal. Each knot equals to 1 3/4 versta, consequently, we covered 196 verstas.

26 June [8 July]. Friday.

Strong gusts of wind were blowing all night long, but by morning the wind began to subside, and the speed of our vessels decreased in proportion to the decrease in wind power. At noon, as usual, it was calculated that we covered 127 knots or 222 verstas in 24 hours. In the afternoon the wind picked up again, and we hoped that if it persists, we will again see coastline whose sight we lost in the German [Northern] Sea.

27 June [9 July]. Saturday.

In the morning we noticed the shores of Denmark. At noon we found that we have sailed another 137 knots (239 verstas). The wind, however, died down in the afternoon, although sea heaving remained strong so that we suffered without moving forward, which was quite frustrating. We could not drop anchor either because of the great depth.

28 June [10 July]. Sunday.

Tailwind has been blowing since 4 o'clock in the morning, but it then turned to headwind, forcing us to maneuver. Since 4 am we only progressed for 50 knots (87 verstas).

29 June [11 July]. Monday.

The same wind direction, we had to constantly maneuver. It was calculated that we covered only 50 knots in 24 hours. We entered the Skagerrak or the Kattegat.[108] At 4:30 pm a calm weather forced us to drop anchor. At 6 pm we set sail, but two hours later, seeing that we could hardly move, we dropped anchor for the night because it was dangerous sailing in a light wind in the Kattegat due to the abundance of shoals that are difficult to avoid with a weak rudder.

30 June [12 July]. Tuesday.

We set sails at 8 o'clock in the morning. The sea was rough, but the wind was fair. However, one circumstance prevented us from develop full speed: it was impossible to put all the sails as the fog did not allow us to see beyond 100 versta [66 miles] distance. Under such conditions it is very dangerous to go in full sail, you may crash with another ship because upon observing it, you may not have enough time to avoid it and collision would be inevitable. Similarly, you can run into shallow waters. In such case, [ships are forced] to reduce speed, fire their guns, ring bells and, in general, produce a lot of noise. We covered another 27 knots (47 verstas) in 24 hours.

The fog has cleared, so we went to full sail but only for a brief period of time. As the wind's strength increased, sails were gradually trimmed and eventually all of them were gone, but we still sailed with incredible speed. For us, who were not sailors, this wind was quite powerful. But a man gets used to everything! While we, sitting in our huge ships, struggled to endure this storm, the Danish boatmen and fishermen on their meager yawls sailed calmly sailed around and approached us offering their services

---

[108] The Skagerrak is a strait running between Norway and the southwest coast of Sweden and the Jutland peninsula of Denmark, connecting the North Sea and the Kattegat sea area, which leads to the Baltic Sea.

as pilots, as well as their herring. Since our ships were deeply immersed in the water, we had to sail through the Great Belt [Storebælt], the deepest of the three straits leading from the Kattegat into the Baltic Sea. We faced a headwind and were unable to maneuver in such confined splace so, at 8 pm, we dropped anchor after making some 80 knots (140 verstas) since 12 pm or 17 1/2 knots per hour.

JULY

1 [13] July. Wednesday.

The sea was still rougher than it was yesterday when the headwinds were blowing which forced us to stand all day at anchor. You can imagine how much we have suffered from the tumbling, without any hope for quick departure. I must say that if we were a little bit further and headed for the Great Belt, we could sail with the wind straight to the Kronstadt.

2 [14] July. Thursday.

Yesterday, about 1 o'clock in the night, while I was still up, the order was issued to raise the anchor. The headwind was still blowing but it was weaker than before and allowed us to undertake some maneuvering. I went to sleep, comforted by the fact that we have finally sailed.

Calculations suggest that we made 20 knots (35 verstas). In these places the coast is very close, so we had an excellent view both on the right and left. In the afternoon a squall blew, but because it was noticed in advance and all sails were cleared in time, we continued to sail safely until 5 pm, when a headwind began to blow again and we were forced to drop anchor. By then, we made 8 knots (14 verstas). If sails are not removed during a squall, the ship could tip over, or the yards, and sometimes the mast, could break. However, if the area has no shoals, such misfortune can be avoided.

3 [15] July. Friday.

Entire day at anchor.

4 [16] July. Saturday.

We set sail at 10 o'clock. The wind was favorable, but, unfortunately, by midday it entirely subsided, and the squadron did not even have time to line up before it was forced to drop anchor.

5 [17] July. Sunday.

At 2 am, when an order was given to weigh anchor, I was still awake. Getting up at 10 o'clock in the morning, I immediately went on deck to see how much we have sailed during the night, but, to my disappointment, I learned that we made only 8 knots. As soon we set sail, the wind began to weaken and we were forced to drop anchor again. At 7 am the wing began to blow once more so we rushed to set sails. We moved incredibly fast, and finally entered the Great Belt, near which we circled for so long unable to enter it. Our voyage lasted until 10 pm, when, owing to the darkness, we had to cast anchor. This Strait has plenty of shoals, and the pilot feared sailing at night, so he decided to anchor ships.

6 [18] July 6. Monday.

We weighed anchor at 3 am and safely passed the most dangerous places in the Belt. The numerous islands, which we passed, are very picturesque. By 5 pm we passed the island of Langeland. Although wind subsided at one moment, it fortunately came back in the evening and we kept moving forward fast.

7 [19] July. Tuesday.

We sailed all night long, leaving the Belt and entering the Baltic Sea. We made 120 knots (210 verstas). Passed Rostock, a seaside town in Mecklenburg. By the evening, our speed decreased as the wind subsided.

8 [20] July. Wednesday.

By 10 am, we observed the island of Borngolm to the right. We sailed 80 knots (140 verstas) in 24 hours. In the afternoon, the wind subsided and we barely moved, although we did sail by Borngolm and Hristianzoe, the fortified islands belonging to Denmark. We sailed about 25 verstas from Hristianzoe, where criminals are exiled. It is so close to Borngolm that it seems as if it was torn away from it and simply floats out in the sea. Both islands present contrasting views. On Borngolm, there are cultivated fields amidst rocks that drew attention of seafarers who are tired of seeing only the sea around them; meanwhile Hristianzoe looks like a pile of stones that were used to build walls with jagged towers, round or square, towering on the water's edge and not allowing to see any ground. I stayed on the deck till night, watching the scenery.

9 [21] July. Thursday.

Waking up and seeing the sea calmer than yesterday, I went back to bed. The heat was incredible, and there was not a single cloud that usually predicts a change in the weather, which we needed so much. However, we still moved and got to the open sea at night. We could see only the sky and sea, calm like an ice sheet. At noon, the wind completely subsided and we felt as if there was not enough air to breathe. Calculations showed that we covered 43.5 knots in 24 hours.

10 [22] July. Friday.

The same weather. Calculations revealed 10 knots (18 verstas) in 24 hours.

11 [23] July. Saturday.

The weather freshened after midnight and, although the wind was not quite fair, we were still moving. We made 65.5 knots (114 verstas) in 24 hours.

12 [24] July. Sunday.

Pleasant sailing. We covered 107 knots (187 verstas) in 24 hours. We now are located between the island of Gotland and the shores of Courland, but could see either of them because we were far from the coast. We hoped to see the first Russian islands - Ösel [Saaremaa Island] and Dago.

13 [25] July. Monday.

At night we saw the island of Ösel and by dawn it disappeared. The wind direction has changed and we have to maneuver. We sailed 65 knots (113 miles and three quarters) in 24 hours.

14 [26] July. Tuesday.

At night the tailwind blew and we passed the island of Dago and entered the Gulf of Finland, which is considered Russian waters. We made 138 verstas. At 5 pm we were near the island of Odensholm. The wind was getting stronger, and our ships were cutting the water with incredible speed. At 8 pm, the wind suddenly changed and forced us to maneuver.

15 [27] July. Wednesday.

Moving with difficulty through the night, our squadron was near Revel this morning when the wind died down. We still had 30 verstas to sail to the port and could see only the highest buildings in the city, the rest of the city hidden behind the horizon; it seemed as if these buildings were separated from the land and had the appearance of islands. Calculations showed that we made 100 verstas in 24 hours. Although very slowly, we still are moving forward and by dawn we reached the island of Wolf and Wrangelsholm and the Koshkarsky lighthouse.

16 [28] July. Thursday.

At night, the tailwind began to blow. We moved about 8 knots per hour and, at 11 o'clock in the morning, reached the Gohland Island where we could distinguish only the mountains, covered with bushes, and no dwellings. Such a spectacle is not particularly attractive, but it seemed divine to us because we knew that only 140 verstas separated us from Kronstadt. We soon observed the Sommersky lighthouse, then Krasnaya gorka at 7 pm and finally Kronstadt itself. A war corvette sailed towards us and upon seeing admiral's flag, it saluted the fleet with cannon shots. The admiral's ship also responded to the salute. Our hearts beat terribly during this ceremony – anyone who has never left his motherland for such a long time, or underwent such hardship and danger for his country, would never understand the excitement we experienced at the sight of our native land. Only those who experienced what we did could easily share sentiments we felt at that moment. At 9 pm, the squadron sailed by the Tolbukhinsky lighthouse and at 10 pm it dropped anchor in the Kronstadt harbor.

17 [29] July. Friday.

At 4 o'clock in the morning we weighed anchor to get closer to Kronstadt, and, at 5 am, anchored next the city. As soon as I got the boat, I went directly to General Potemkin on the Jupiter to deliver my report and then got to Kronstadt to send batman to St Petersburg, and returned to dine on the ship.

Conclusion

The happiness that I felt upon finding myself so close to my loved ones after a 28-month long absence and so fortunately escaping so many perils and adventures quite naturally led me to forsake my diary which I so painstakingly kept from March 9, 1812 on July 17, 1814 After recovering from all the excitement caused by returning home, I felt obliged to describe, however briefly, how we arrived in St. Petersburg, without specifying days or dates which I [would have] completely confused. So here are a few words how it all happened.

A few days after arriving in Kronstadt, we were landed at Oranienbaum where we took up quarters. As soon as I stepped ashore, I found myself in front of [Mikhail] Bakunin (the governor of St. Petersburg) with Bibikov, and together we traveled to St. Petersburg. Along the way, since we happened to pass the house where Bakunin's family lived, I could not refuse seeing it and actually spent a couple very pleasant hours there. Arriving finally in St. Petersburg, I could not get a meeting with Madame B. and immediately noticed a change in our relationship. Then I surprised my sisters with my sudden appearance at 11 o'clock in the evening. Their joy was indescribable. The following day I returned to Oranienbaum and settled in a disgusting village. The Empress Mother [Maria Fedorovna] arranged a lovely celebration for us at Pavlovsk and we were transported on court horses because we had none left. After everything we had seen [in Europe], the festivity at Pavlovsk did not dazzle us but it affected us otherwise - it touched us to the depths of our hearts. I will never forget the attention shown to us by Great Duchess Anna[109] and all the praise she shared with me.

Sometime later, we changed quarters and moved closer to St. Petersburg along the Peterhof Road. I had to stay with [Ivan] Pushin, the chief naval quartermaster. This deployment did not last long, and in August we entered the capital, passing underneath the Triumphal Arc that

---

[109] Emperor Alexander's sister and future queen of Netherlands

was constructed some time ago.[110] The entire Imperial family was present on that day, but, in general, the welcome we received in St. Petersburg was much more subdued than the receptions we got in Dresden and Paris.

---

[110] The Triumphal Arc, also known as the Narva Gates was a wooden structure constructed on the Narva highway with the purpose of greeting the soldiers who were returning from abroad after their victory over Napoleon. The architect of the original Narva Gate was Giacomo Quarenghi, who designed it after the Arc de Triomphe du Carrousel in Paris, originally erected to celebrate Napoleon's victory over the Allies at Austerlitz.

Made in the USA
Monee, IL
16 May 2021